I0062598

Praise for *Team Harmony*

'People are the most complex system on the planet. Leading and managing people is difficult, challenging work. Ilona Vass introduces an exquisite metaphor, harmony, to guide us intelligently and practically on the vagaries, variances, and variety needed to lead and manage teams successfully. I've read hundreds of books on this stuff. *Team Harmony* is a stand-out. Ilona elegantly and eloquently packs an enormous practical punch into *Team Harmony* that gave me guidance and wisdom in practical measures. If you lead a team, learn from Ilona Vass. Bravo.'

COLIN JAMES Co-Founder, Colin James Method, 2020 Australian Keynote Speaker of the Year, 2008 Australian Educator of the Year

'*Team Harmony* is a must-read for mid-level managers navigating today's intricate workplace dynamics. This book offers a holistic approach to leadership that goes beyond traditional management books. The concept of striking the right chord within teams is brilliantly explored, and the case studies provide relatable examples that drive home the principles. If you seek a roadmap to lead with empathy and clarity and positively impact team dynamics, then *Team Harmony* is a valuable and unique addition to your leadership bookshelf.'

WAYNE PEARCE OAM Wayne Pearce Advantage, NRL Legend, Hall of Fame Top 100 Players

‘I love how Ilona Vass has layered *Team Harmony* using music as the canvas for leadership, communication and collaboration. The blank canvas of music is silence. Notes layered on the canvas create melody, harmony and resolution interspersed with discord and bare silence. It’s the perfect metaphor for middle managers seeking to create and sustain team harmony. Equally perfect is the way Vass presents ideas and concepts that are deep on practicality, with exercises clearly segmented to make this a book for pragmatic managers making greater progress through better communication with their team. Like music, I feel it deepens communication to touch our souls. Communication that brings people together more than words ever can. This book gifts you the best of Ilona’s experience here in your hand.’

DR. RICHARD HODGE This Century Thinking & Design Expert, Mentor’s Mentor, Thought Leaders Business School, Faculty Member

The Only Communication Playbook You Need

‘What I love about *Team Harmony* is the commonsense guidance it provides that’s grounded in sound research, observations and first-hand experience of the author. The musical metaphor and three-element model are accessible and relatable, providing managers in the modern workplace with the tools and techniques to drive better team dynamics. The real-world examples of miscommunication, their impact and ways to fix them brought the Resonance, Consonance, Dissonance model to life. If you're a people leader looking for inspiration to refresh or upgrade your communication skills, this is the only playbook you'll need.'

PAUL SCOTT General Manager, LMS365

Orchestrating Leadership Excellence

'*Team Harmony* is a must-read for mid-level managers navigating today's intricate workplace dynamics. The author's deep understanding of mid-level managers' challenges shines through every page. The concept of striking the right chord within teams is brilliantly explored. The emphasis on fostering harmony within teams resonated with me, and the actionable techniques and strategies have already yielded positive results in my leadership journey. *Team Harmony* is your transformational tool if you're eager to create a harmonious and high-performing team.'

ADA CHENG CEO, Australian Nursing Home Foundation (ANHF)

'*Team Harmony* offers crucial guidance for mid-senior-level managers navigating the intricate landscape of cross-cultural diversity within the global workplace. Highlighting the pivotal link between diversity and success, the book not only acknowledges the challenges but also provides invaluable insights on cultivating harmonious cultures. Through a skilful narrative, the author understands the delicate balance required to lead teams to success by crafting a harmonious contemporary workspace. A truly enlightening read, *Team Harmony* is an essential resource for anyone seeking to leave a profound impact in diverse workplaces.'

SACHIN KHISTI Managing Director, Carrington Associates

TEAM HARMONY

TEAM HARMONY

Striking the Right Chord — A Guide for Leading People in the Modern Workplace

ILONA VASS

GRAMMAR FACTORY
— ESTᴰ 2013 —

Published by Grammar Factory Publishing, an imprint of MacMillan Company Limited.

Grammar Factory Publishing
MacMillan Company Limited
25 Telegram Mews, 39th Floor, Suite 3906
Toronto, Ontario, Canada
M5V 3Z1

www.grammarfactory.com

Vass, Ilona
Team Harmony: Striking the Right Chord — A Guide for Leading People in the Modern Workplace / Ilona Vass.

Paperback ISBN 978-1-998756-43-8
Hardcover ISBN 978-1-998756-45-2
eBook ISBN 978-1-998756-44-5

1. BUS103000 BUSINESS & ECONOMICS / Organisational Development. 2. BUS071000 BUSINESS & ECONOMICS / Leadership. 3. BUS041000 BUSINESS & ECONOMICS / Management.

Production Credits
Cover design by Designerbility
Interior layout design by Setareh Ashrafologhalai
Book production and editorial services by Grammar Factory Publishing

Grammar Factory's Carbon Neutral Publishing Commitment
Grammar Factory Publishing is proud to be neutralising the carbon footprint of all printed copies of its authors' books printed by or ordered directly through Grammar Factory or its affiliated companies through the purchase of Gold Standard-Certified International Offsets.

As the author of this book, I wish to acknowledge that Aboriginal and Torres Strait Islander peoples are the Traditional Custodians and the first storytellers of the lands on which I live and work and where this book was written. I want to honour their continuous connection and commitment to Country, water, skies and communities and pay respect to Elders in all realms of time.

CONTENTS

OVERTURE[1]

THE LIGHTS ARE about to go out...

I am sitting in an upper gallery of the Vienna State Opera, joined by my teenage son and my mother. We excitedly wait for the beginning of an evening of indulgence. A live music performance always gives me unique happiness and enjoyment. And I can't wait for the performance to start.

I soak it all in.

There is the murmuring sound of chatter from all the audience members. They are, like me, waiting for the opera to start, using the time to talk to each other about this and that.

The architecture is overwhelmingly beautiful. As I have refreshed my memory before this evening, the Vienna State Opera was built from 1861 to 1869 in the Neo-Renaissance style. It was initially called 'Vienna Court Opera' (Wiener Hofoper) and changed later to 'Vienna State Opera' (Wiener Staatsoper) after Austria became a republic.

The building has quite a tragic history and was not very popular with the Viennese population then. Due to some city building mishaps, the opera was not fully visible and appeared to be 'sunk' from a street view.

The story goes that Emperor Franz Joseph I (Kaiser Franz Joseph) had made a critical remark about the visual appearance of the opera, and the devastated architect Eduard van der Nüll committed suicide after that before the building was finished and officially opened. Kaiser Franz Joseph was so shocked that he never allowed himself to publicly say anything except *'Es war sehr schoen; es hat mich sehr gefreut' ('It was very nice; I was delighted')*.

I have a great view from above in the gallery, and the activity in the orchestra pit catches my attention. The orchestra is placed in a lowered area before the stage in opera or ballet performances.

I can see the small individual lamps for every musician shining a light on their musical notes.

There are many different instruments. I can make out the violins, violas and cellos, a couple of flutes, horns and bassoons, two timpani and a harp.

I also hear a cacophony of instrumental sounds mixed with the audience chatter. It's an entanglement of pitches and notes, and is excitingly chaotic. Some musicians are practising particular passages from the opera ahead. I guess they are the tricky ones. Some seem to look through their musical notes quietly, some share a quick laugh with a colleague, while others sit still. I can't see if they have their eyes closed, but I could imagine that they are meditating or practising to gain a last-minute focus on what lies ahead.

While the lights are getting dimmed until they are turned off, the cacophony in the orchestra pit stops. There is this brief rise in the excitement as everyone in the audience says a final 'Ah, it's starting' before all talking stops.

Complete silence.

Everyone looks at the orchestra pit, waiting for the curtains to open.

Applause! The conductor comes out of the backstage area with verve and panache. He is making his way to the elevated conductor's desk, the spotlight following him. At his desk, he turns to the audience and bows.

Then he swirls around, making eye contact with all the different orchestra sections.

Everyone seems to take a deep breath in, holding it...

This is the moment of the orchestra!

With undivided attention, the audience stares at them. The first piece of every opera, the overture, is performed by only the orchestra before their role changes and they collaborate with the singers on stage.

Singers can't see the orchestra, only the conductor, who is the all-important link between what's happening on stage and his team of musicians.

The conductor raises his baton...

And then there is harmony.

PRELUDE

'You need to know so much more than just how to wave your arms around. You need to read everything you can get your hands on to be able to grow into a fine conductor. You have to have so much knowledge in every area that is more than music.'

RICCARDO MUTI ON WHAT IT MEANS TO BE A CONDUCTOR

WHEN I WAS at the Vienna State Opera in June 2022, listening to the opera *The Magic Flute (Zauberfloete)* by Mozart, I not only enjoyed a wonderful time, but I also had an experience that would unconsciously influence me to create some of the concepts in this book.

During the performance, I had the epiphany that an orchestra and their conductor are an excellent analogy for a team and their leader in the workplace. That was not a new analogy, as I discovered in my research later, but I found it was worth exploring further.

A conductor is not only directing the orchestra; they are also the link between the singer on stage and the orchestra. A mid-level or frontline manager, or a team or department leader, is precisely that – the connection between the employees and the senior management level in a company.

And it's a position that can be challenging, especially in today's dynamic business environment and the new forms of working, like hybrid and remote work.

Take Joe, for example.

Joe is a middle manager in his company's people and culture department with a team of twenty-five people. Joe was promoted last year to this role. He works on improving workplace culture by embracing diversity, fostering psychological safety[2], and having all employees' wellbeing at heart.

His current challenges are around the people management side of things. Joe's team is very diverse. Not only culturally but also in terms of work scenarios. Joe's company has a flexible work model, which creates challenges. There has also been quite a bit of staff turnover since the pandemic and Joe struggles with a constantly understaffed team and a high workload.

While he feels that most of his team is great, there are two or three team members he struggles with. Joe has tried different approaches. He tried to be understanding, and he tried to be authoritative. But the conversations didn't go well, and he feels these team members disrespect his leadership. They disturb the team's efforts and create tension among the other employees. Because of that, power struggles are going on among some employees, and whingeing and gossip distract people from their work.

Joe's biggest frustration is that he cannot bring harmony to the team. He would love to get the smouldering undercurrents under control so everyone can work efficiently. With the new flexible work options, his department has to implement many changes, and he feels overwhelmed. Joe is concerned that his superiors, who put him into this role, feel disappointed with his leadership and have started doubting his capabilities.

Joe feels the need to be better equipped for his role but does not get the support he needs. Putting out fires all the time, getting more and more things to do from his superiors, and seeing good people leave takes its toll on him.

He has heard rumours that others see him as overcontrolling; he knows he is sometimes impatient, and even at home he is not his best self. Joe feels a bit like a failure and has caught himself googling symptoms of burnout.

He wishes he had more tools and knowledge to handle different people better. His first wish is to know how to communicate with difficult people effectively and confidently.

He really longs for more harmony within his team. To use a musical metaphor, he wishes he could perform like an orchestra conductor, with his team working under his guidance to create beautiful, harmonious music.

The challenges of modern middle management

Joe's experience is not unusual for middle managers. Middle management is often described as a sandwich position, and can be challenging for myriad reasons. For example:

- You must decide how to communicate with both your employee teams and senior management so that things can move forward.
- You must keep an overview of how your teams work and if the company strategies are implemented and executed.
- You must handle demands and stress on both sides to protect the 'performance'.

This all demands a skill set you may have not fully developed when you take on your role as a mid-level manager (or conductor), especially if you have recently been promoted to such a role for the first time. It is the human equation[3]! You may feel happy about the promotion and overwhelmed by the new responsibilities – ambivalence is normal.

While the 'sandwich' position of mid-level and frontline management is not new, these managers often feel even more stuck between executive and employee expectations in the modern workplace. The pressure hasn't eased at all. On the contrary, if anything, it has increased. These people have seen a massive shift in their responsibilities and how their teams are coping and functioning. And they are only sometimes sure that they have adapted adequately.

The latest research (Microsoft's 2022 Work Trend Index) has established that forty-three per cent of leaders say relationship building is the greatest challenge in remote and hybrid work. It is more difficult with remote workers, as well as employees who were hired during the pandemic. In addition, sixty-two per cent of leaders are concerned that new employees aren't getting the support they need and feel out of their depth and out of resources. The report also discovered that fifty-four per cent of company leaders worldwide have to be in touch with employee expectations. Furthermore, seventy-one per cent of middle managers

(MMs) in Australia (seventy-four per cent globally) say they have no influence or resources to make necessary changes on behalf of their teams.

Another study by Boston Consulting Group called MMs a '*neglected but critical group*' for driving success at their firms. To make hybrid work a success, MMs need to be empowered to establish new practices for sustainable and flexible work, rebuild social capital for digital-first teams and foster them to be culture keepers.

Most importantly, MMs have to ensure their teams are safe in all aspects. Safe from being overworked and sliding into burnout, safe from psychological stress and even warfare, and safe in addressing challenges and making mistakes.

My own research backs up these findings. In my preparation for this book, I interviewed MMs from various industries and different parts of Australia, and what they shared with me are some crucial questions leaders ask themselves nowadays:

1. How do I onboard and integrate new team members effectively?

2. How do I do this fast when we have an increased staff turnover?

3. What can I do to make my team feel like a team, although we hardly see each other in person?

4. How do I establish meaningful relationships with and within hybrid and remote teams?

5. How can I make meetings more effective without jeopardising the human equation?

6. How can I build trust fast?

7. What can I do to improve communication and foster accountability?

8. Finally, how do I connect my hybrid and remote teams to the organisation's fabric?

It's clear that MMs face a new and urgent challenge. They have to manage their teams in a way that balances the expectations for flexible work and business outcomes. This requires new skills in leading people and more freedom and trust from the executive level.

Your executive level may currently be outsourcing 'how to handle the practical side of work flexibility' to middle management and team leaders. So, the daily operation of dispersed team members and the variety of combinations of how the team functions as a productive, successful and harmonious entity are left to you.

Your team members will rely on you to create a work environment that allows them to do their best work, considering individual working styles. They rely on you to communicate coherently so they feel heard and understood and, regardless of the location, feel they are an important part of the team. They will seek guidance when conflict arises and hope you can navigate the disturbances. Do you feel equipped and ready for this?

You may feel you lack knowledge about how to deal with negative human behaviour, or how to communicate, handle conflict or motivate your team to do their best. And you don't want to be an unpopular, aggressive, overbearing manager, or indeed a weak and meek manager who doesn't know how to create harmony within the team in this new and challenging environment.

What is harmony?

'Harmony and improved team performance are rooted in positive focus, a commitment to excellence, and ongoing mutual trust and respect.'

TERRY ORLICK

In Pursuit of Excellence

We often say, 'In peace and harmony'. But what does that actually mean? And what does team harmony encompass? Indeed, is team harmony truly beneficial?

Some argue that 'playing nice and being friendly all the time' can slow down teams, and that teamwork should be provocative and challenging. This understanding of harmony is sometimes found in companies whose motto is 'We don't do conflict', thereby overly emphasising positivity and neglecting hard conversations by labelling them as 'negative'.

Some speak of false team harmony, which can create destructive undercurrents that might have the opposite effect of a team in real harmony. They believe that superficial harmony supports the pretence of being friendly and peaceful, though, under the table, team members form secret factions and gossip about each other, even sabotaging each other in subtle and manipulative ways.

Others see a significant benefit in team harmony. Business success is measurable and rewarding when you, as a people-leader, can establish and maintain team harmony despite the constant flux of team dynamics and the fast changes to the team members in hybrid, blended and remote settings.

This is when team harmony has a broader meaning, emphasising communication, acceptance of differences in all forms, and true collaboration. It is this broader meaning of harmony that is of interest to you as a people-leader.

Just like Joe, you are a people-leader. I use the term 'people-leader' because it does not define a particular role or position within a company. You might be a middle manager, a department head, a mid-level manager, a team leader, a frontline group captain, or even a senior manager. But what all people-leaders have in common is that they are responsible for a group of people and have the noble task of influencing how the individual people work together positively, with compassion and harmony. In the spirit of the Greek root word, ἁρμονία, harmony means 'agreement'.

So, you could say people are in harmony when they sing or play together and agree to do so. In relation to the work world, you could say that harmony is the agreement of people to work together with the aspiration of an outcome. And you, as a people-leader, will want to support this and aspire to establish team harmony.

Understanding how harmony is created in music deepens and expands our understanding of how to create harmony in the workplace. In music, it is a misconception that harmony is simply something that 'sounds nice'. Yes, the harmony might be pleasing, and that is called Consonance. But an essential part of harmony in music is Dissonance, which creates musical tension. So, there is the idea of a harmonic progression, where a series of Consonance and Dissonance make a complete thought (or pleasing melody). This is the common understanding of harmony in western music.

In other words, there can't be harmony without at one point having a Dissonance. The Dissonance will be musically 'resolved' and moves back into Consonance. And this happens a few times. In my last choir concert performance, we sang a piece that was challenging to us in the beginning, as it had quite a few chords that made us think we were singing it wrong. But it was exactly that Dissonance that would point us to the harmony in the chord afterwards. Practising this piece more and more made us embrace the Dissonance more and we understood why it was there.

For you as a people-leader, it will be in your interest to do all it takes to have your team in harmony. This is a big task! people-leaders have to become conductors for orchestras that are both present and invisible – with some musicians working in person, some at odd times, and others virtually. Are you prepared to establish a 'team feeling' for all these musicians? Are you ready to adapt communication to ensure this? Do you feel empowered to handle misalignments, conflicts and other mishaps, so that team harmony is not jeopardised?

'Empowering managers to adapt to new employee expectations helps set businesses up for long-term success.'

JARED SPATARO

CVP, Modern Work, Microsoft

Libretto[4]

My intention with this book is to help you deal with the challenges of being a manager in a modern workplace. I will provide you with insights, help and practical tips to create and maintain harmony in your team. This book is a guide to ease the pressure of managing multiple people in your day-to-day work. With the tools presented in the pages to come, you can step fully into your leadership without massive stress and anxiety.

Based on the concept of harmony in music, I have created a model that will give you a quick diagnostic of how you and your team are functioning and what you must correct or address to achieve a state of team harmony. This model reflects a fluent process that constantly balances *Resonance*, *Dissonance* and *Consonance*. These components together, like in music, build the base of a constant 'vibration' that we perceive as harmony.

Like an opera, this book is split into three distinct Acts: *Act I - Resonance*, *Act II - Dissonance* and *Act III - Consonance*. Each Act will equip you with different skills to be able to achieve harmony in any of your teams, as well as highlight two important factors to focus on.

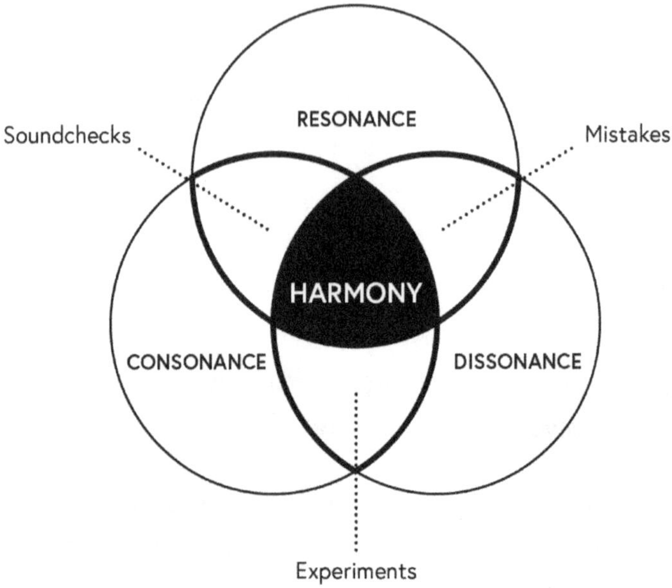

Let me return to the orchestra analogy and music theory to explain what these Acts mean, what they will teach you, and how each is successfully achieved.

Act I - Resonance

To deliver an amazing performance, the musicians first come together, finding a general Resonance or collaboration with each other. This happens long before they sit in the orchestra pit on the night of the performance. The violinists sit together, the percussionists reside in the back part of the orchestra with their many instruments, where they take up quite some space, and you can hear the clarinettists tuning their instruments.

The orchestra members know and agree that they will work together, know what is expected, and work out how best to perform – all under the guidance of the conductor. They have clear expectations and an idea of how to meet them.

In this Act, you will learn how to onboard new team members, how to establish great team communication and what is important in communication, especially if you have a hybrid work environment.

Act II – Dissonance

Next, the musicians practise passages of the music from their upcoming performance. They might do this individually or in small groups. When practising and working together, there can be a cacophony of sounds, high and low notes, trills and thumps. This is Dissonance, when the musicians tumble through challenges, experiment with sound and learn what works through failure or mistakes.

They might sometimes disagree over ideas on how to play specific passages. They might be frustrated when someone makes the same mistake over and over again. They might feel impatient with the progress and vocalise it. Have you ever heard a musician 'torturing' their instrument to let the frustration out?

This Act will teach you about the energy created in conflict and how to best utilise it. I will also look at the concept of stepping into conflict and experimenting to be able to move out of Dissonance and into harmony.

Act III - Consonance

Finally, the orchestra is ready for the performance despite challenges and hurdles. They have a last practise in the orchestra pit to do their soundchecks. Then there is silence, anticipation and excitement. Everyone is prepared, ready and in complete sync. The team is in Consonance.

In this Act, you will learn how to maintain your team in harmony and what the benefits are when your team is in Consonance.

Maintaining your team in Consonance will require you to keep observing the company and team *culture*. As their leader, you must reinforce all traits that support harmony and lead by example. I will give you examples and tools on what is important to do to keep up the Consonance.

If you look at the model again, you will see three subsections where each Act overlaps with another - Mistakes, Experiments and Soundchecks. These additional signposts indicate transitions that you and your team will experience, and are where you will find opportunities for your team to grow and ensure you are creating harmony.

When team members make *mistakes*, there is a possibility that you will experience Dissonance. Such mistakes can be of any kind, like technical errors, behavioural 'stray bullets' and administrative glitches.

Finding the courage to undertake *experiments* to work on the Dissonance in your team – to help them deal with conflicts productively and prevent your team getting stuck in drama – is not for the faint-hearted. Here your leadership is tested substantially, and your team will wait for your guidance to re-establish the desired harmony.

Once your team is in Consonance, you will be required to do regular *soundchecks* on the team harmony. It is easy to miss small signs that team harmony is becoming wobbly if no soundchecks are conducted.

In the book, you will also notice multiple *arias*[5], which are exercises designed to help you understand how the theories in every Act can be applied to real-life scenarios. The *Recitatives*[6] throughout this book identify special case stories of people like you whom I have worked with to successfully achieve harmony in their teams, as well as personal stories from my corporate career.

I will present you with heuristic tools in each Act that help you understand where your team is and, if necessary, what you can do to intervene quickly and establish team harmony. When I talk about heuristic tools, I mean a philosophy of leadership you can use to achieve harmony by trial and error as the conductor of your team.

I am very drawn to heuristic principles, as they step away from a dogmatic 'this is what you must do' approach. Heuristic tools supply you with quickly applicable methods to cut through the noise and regain harmony. They will guide you to conduct the orchestra in the right direction, and support you so the musicians keep playing the right notes.

> 'Heuristic principles are not guaranteed to be optimal or perfect but are sufficient to reach an intermediate goal; they are rules of thumb that we know are imperfect, but that simplify things and make them easier to implement.'
>
> **DR PAIGE WILLIAMS**
>
> *Becoming AntiFragile*

By implementing these tools and techniques, you will feel well-prepared for challenging situations, and know what to observe and what interventions to set, so your team can work in harmony for success and productivity. Your reputation as a confident leader will grow, and you will become a trusted pillar in your organisation.

By following the philosophy and guidance in this book, you will begin to see your team's many different personalities and behaviours as potential strengths for you to explore rather than a problem or threat. You will learn tools and strategies for any bumps in the road.

So, are you ready to achieve team harmony?

'You don't get harmony when everybody sings the same note.'

SOURCE UNKNOWN

ACT I

RESONANCE

'In this world, everything has a pulse or a vibration. This sound is unique to each living or non-living thing and in itself creates a music that no one can hear. I believe that this has a very powerful resonance with, and a deep effect on, our lives.'

MIKE OLDFIELD

THE TITLE OF this book is 'Team Harmony', and the goal of this book is to help you, the people-leader, achieve harmony in your team. But this is neither a quick nor simple task. Just as an orchestra must spend hours in rehearsal and practise, practise, practise, so too must a corporate team take a journey towards harmony. So, where to start that journey? Just as with an orchestra, achieving harmony starts with Resonance.

The key themes of this chapter are communication and connection. Resonance in the form of good communication and connection is essential to team harmony. It is the starting point, the base, or the framework.

We will explore the dangers of poor communication and non-existing connections, and we will look at techniques that will help you improve these aspects. Think of communication as the expression of a team member's voice, and connection as the deep listening that ensures that a voice is heard.

So, how does this process of expression and listening begin? In this phase, as with the musicians of an orchestra, a team comes to work together and starts with a general collaboration. The process of sharing ideas begins, and projects and goals are discussed.

To help you do this, I'd like to share the first Aria of the book. The Team Charter is an exercise that helps you as the leader set the direction for a team and allows the individual team members to do so safely and in a structured way. Think of this as the stage for your team's performance or the foundation of your success.

ARIA: TEAM CHARTER

Here are the steps for conducting the Team Charter exercise:

1. First, as a team, discuss and agree on the team's purpose, values, goals and expected behaviours. Then, encourage each team member to share their thoughts and opinions openly and respectfully. If you have team members who are shy or have culturally conformed statements, suggest writing things down individually before discussing them.

2. Set the expectation that everyone will contribute.

3. Dig deeper into what team members will come up with. For example, they might say, 'Listen to what others have to say and let everyone speak without interruption.'

4. Ask them, 'How does that look for you? How do I know that you are listening to me? What cues do you give me so I can be sure?' This ensures that different personalities express what a particular Charter item actually means for them. It diminishes misunderstanding and superficialities.

5. Record the team's agreements in a shared document and possibly on a whiteboard.

6. Review the team's agreements regularly, such as at the beginning of each important meeting or the start of each project.

7. Hold team members accountable for upholding the team's agreements.

Later in the book we will revisit this idea, but now let's delve more deeply into the key themes of this chapter: communication and connection. There have been recent and extreme changes to the Resonance of teams and employees for a people-leader. The pandemic and its reverberation have uprooted the structure of group work, how teams are formed and how they communicate. Communication and connections are two key areas where disruption to Resonance can occur.

Communication

Communication is relevant for all three elements of team harmony, but especially in this Resonance phase. It is in this phase that you establish the tune for your team culture.

Good communication involves both speaking up and being listened to. It is a two-way street. Without this flow and acceptance of information, company culture can become toxic. One of my clients had a boss whose communication style featured the statement: 'Don't come to me with problems. Come to me with solutions.' In other words, this boss refused to listen. My client said the dismissal of people's problems, which often involved interpersonal conflict, indicated acceptance of bad behaviour from the organisation's leadership. Ultimately she decided to leave the company. Her argument was that the company is not worth hanging around if she can't do her work properly and the leader doesn't want to hear about it.

It might be tempting to view such a scenario as a personality clash, but I don't think that was the problem. In fact, research by Google's Project Aristotle supports this. The tech giant conducted internal research involving more than 100 teams over many years in an endeavour to discover what made the 'perfect' team.

'We looked at 180 teams from all over the company. We had lots of data, but nothing showed that a mix of specific personality types, skills, or backgrounds made any difference. The "who" part of the equation didn't seem to matter.'

ABEER DUBEY

Director, People Analytics, Google

What did contribute to making the team successful was emotional safety *and equal contribution to the conversation*, regardless of intersectionality. In other words, good communication – being able to express an opinion without fear and knowing you will be heard – is a proven example of what brings a team closer to 'perfect'.

It was so interesting to realise that who is in the group is less important than how the members interact with each other. When the group communicated in trusting ways and were allowed to show emotions, the team was productive, innovative and successful. I encourage all people-leaders to keep an open communication flow in mind when starting to work with a team, especially if it's a new team, or one that is actively recruiting new members into its fold.

Let's take onboarding a new team member as an example.

Sabine, one of my former students, was super enthusiastic about landing a role as marketing assistant in a reputable company. On her first day, she was ready! She wanted to prove herself and show her boss that she was willing to learn fast and work hard. On her first day, she shook a lot of hands, got many smiles and was shown her workstation. The first week went by quickly; the first month was okay, though she felt a bit left on her own.

She started to feel embarrassed that she had to ask her colleagues so many things and 'muddled' her way through, making a series of mistakes due to her lack of knowledge of the company structure or where to get information. She was unclear how and to whom to communicate certain things and where to get approval for her work, as different superiors criticised her for not showing her work to them but to another superior.

Over the trial period, Sabine became anxious. She was trying to avoid mistakes and not annoy her colleagues with too many questions. But she was at a loss as to how to improve things and lost her enthusiasm for the job she always wanted.

This example of one-way communication is unfortunately not an uncommon practice. It results in high staff turnover, and creates a lack of trust and limitations to good collaboration. Team harmony is far away!

Reading your team's music

Learning how to communicate effectively is like learning how to read music; it takes time and effort, but once you know how, you can play almost anything. It's exactly the same for you and your team.

I am deeply passionate about good communication in the workplace. It is the main focus of my work, and the experiences my clients share with me confirm that all types of mid-level managers and team leaders need help with getting team communication right from the very start of their careers.

Here are some questions to help you reflect on your personal communication style:

- Does my way of communication represent a 'fair and square' or equitable style?

- How do I connect with all my team members?
- How can I make what I say have impact?
- How can I prevent catastrophic misinterpretations?
- How can I cut through the noise and mixed messages to better understand the people on my team?
- Are my current strategies working, or do they keep failing?
- How can I trust that my internal communication plans will work?

Suppose you believe that your communication style could be improved. In that case, you may like to familiarise yourself with the Process Communication Model (PCM), discovered by psychologist Dr Taibi Kahler, which I believe is the most profound communication tool in use today. It encourages people to expand and tap into their full communication potential, which is often dormant and underutilised.

PCM looks at the communication process and stipulates that *how* we say something is often more important than *what* we say. PCM encourages you to see that you have the potential to communicate well, even with people who are very different from you. When I am coaching clients, I encourage them not to look at different types *of* people and communication styles but rather at all the different people and communication styles *in* themselves. It is a fantastic tool for aligning team communication with all members, existing and new.

When working with people-leaders and their teams, the communication process is always a key element for improvement. My clients often say they wish they had known and learned about this tool earlier. I often get their feedback on how their connection with a difficult colleague has dramatically improved by applying their newly gained knowledge. Teams have a new basis for communicating with each other and often establish innovative ways to work together. They know how to support each other's different communication needs and preferences.

Communication agility is what you, as a people-leader, will want to choose in order to connect with people better and faster. Your team members will also *resonate* with each other better. For a people-leader like you, that means assessing your team members' communication preferences (reading the music of your team members), connecting with them using the language they understand and resonate with, and motivating them in individual ways so they can perform at their best.

This works equally well with team members of different generations, as this communication approach looks at the human core and human behaviour rather than promoting generalisations about Gen X, Y or Z.

Let communication become your most significant leadership asset, and everything else will fall into place.

RECITATIVE: HEINZ

Would you agree that everyday work communication is often the biggest hurdle to team harmony and success and can immensely frustrate people-leaders? This is particularly true for how we work in the post-pandemic world, with hybrid and remote work forms, blended teams and new demands on MMs from the executive level.

Heinz, one of my clients in Austria, said that his life as a mid-level manager in an IT company had become much more complicated when the firm introduced hybrid working. Heinz manages a sales team of fourteen employees, with half working from home when they are not with clients and half working from the office when they are not with clients.

He told me that he suddenly feels he is dealing with two different teams, and it is hard to bring them all together. When a date suits everyone, they mostly meet on Zoom. Heinz said that communication got much more complicated, and miscommunication increased; this caused a lot of stress, overwork and even burnout.

Heinz was desperate to find ways to reconnect and communicate better. He knew he had to up his game as a leader and learn more about motivating people while considering different working and communication preferences.

When working with Heinz, we created a plan for what he had to discover about his team members to function better. A series of questions was sent to them, and their responses gave Heinz great insight into the different needs of each team member. The aspiration for Heinz and his team was to become an A-team.

We also looked at Heinz's 'communication saboteurs' and established what he would need from his team as their leader. To his surprise, everyone was on board. Heinz established a 'visibility board' for the team members. He checked in with them more often, getting updates on progress and what they needed from him to do not only their individual work but teamwork, too. Heinz established non-monetary team goals outside the individual sales goals in a collaborative workshop I facilitated. These goals were important for everyone and were fun to achieve. Needless to say, they built trust and strong connections.

With these measures, Heinz was able to make hybrid work for him as well as for his team.

To get the Resonance part of team harmony working best, focus on improving everyday communication at work. Get to know your team's different communication styles and make a good communication culture a priority for everyone on your team.

Understanding communication styles

The fastest way to build a connection with another human being is to understand their communication preferences. These preferences can include the following:

1. The form of communication: do they like email, text, chat forums, phone calls, Snapchat, video conversations, etc.?

2. The communication style: what is their preferred perception, their way of viewing the world and their way of exchanging these views with others? This will

shape their communication and even their preferred vocabulary.

3. The communication interaction: people mostly use four different communication methods. Based on the PCM, there are four basic interaction styles: Ask, Care, Play and Tell.

    a. **ASK:** This interaction is significant in the work world. It requires exchanging information and data, checking in with others, and getting approvals in democratic ways. It is requestive in nature.

    b. **CARE:** This interaction involves emotions, feelings, empathy and compassion. There is an interest in others and the desire to make everyone comfortable. It fosters a more profound connection on a human level and is nurturing in nature.

    c. **PLAY:** This interaction is humorous, uplifting and animated. It can provide an outlet for serious situations, lighten the mood, and bring an 'oomph' to dull and tedious tasks. It is emotive in nature.

    d. **TELL:** This interaction is interested in getting things moving. With clear instructions, even commands, actions are set into motion and objectives are pursued. It is directive in nature.

When working with clients, I explain these four communication interactions and then let them reflect on their preferences. Is there something missing in the team communication? Are all interactions present in meetings?

ARIA: COMMUNICATING WELL WITH YOUR TEAM FROM THE GET-GO

Use these tips to assist you in communicating with your team members:

- Assess your leadership communication potential by observing what communication style makes you tired, switched off or frustrated. This is a good indicator that you do not easily access that particular communication style and don't understand it. You've discovered a blind spot! With the right knowledge, you can improve this dormant communication style and connect with people who might be communicating very differently. Ask your team members the following questions:
    - What do you prefer my communication style to be?

- How do I/we know when things are not going well for you, and you need help?
- What does 'being clear' mean for you?
- How do I invite you to contribute to a meeting?
- How do you want me to check in with you on work progress?

- Establish a 'communicate with each other' approach that is team-led.
- Incorporate this in your meetings too.

Check out the Leadership Communication Potential Package on my website for an in-depth assessment and debrief.

Connection

In the bustling realm of the workplace, connection serves as the lifeblood that fuels productivity and nurtures a thriving environment. It is the intangible force that forges bonds between individuals, fostering collaboration, trust and a sense of belonging.

While artificial intelligence (AI) has revolutionised numerous aspects of our lives, it cannot replicate the profound impact of human connection. AI excels in processing vast amounts of data, automating repetitive tasks and providing insights. However, it lacks the empathetic understanding, emotional intelligence and nuanced interpersonal skills that are essential for fostering genuine connections and building meaningful relationships.

The inherent human ability to empathise, communicate and connect on a deeper level remains irreplaceable, anchoring the workplace in the rich tapestry of human interaction.

Do you remember the Team Charter exercise from earlier? This exercise will shape how you hold your meetings and how new team members will be guided to find their way within the group, especially in any onboarding process. The beauty of this exercise is that it creates a formal setting for team members to connect. The team sits together and, guided by rules, everyone is encouraged to express themselves. Further, those rules keep them safe while they do so. This exercise is a great resource for establishing good connections as the team moves into Resonance.

Leading by example

There is no way around it. As a modern people-leader, you will show how you trust your team by example. You will support and create an atmosphere of openness with all team members through clear and inclusive communication, deepening the group's connections.

Let's look at some ways to do that.

ARIA: LEADING BY EXAMPLE

When introducing team members to each other, add something personal that makes people relatable. For example: 'This is Nancy, the team leader for our procurement team, and she is a wizard in the kitchen. She loves to cook Vietnamese, and we love tasting her food at our year-end gathering.'

When introducing a new team member, or re-inventing your current team's connection, ask each member the following:

- What does a productive meeting look like for you?
- How do you prefer to contribute to the team discussion?
- What can I do to be a better team leader next month?

- What is missing from our team?
- What did we do well as a team last week?

Schedule time for regular one-on-one conversations with each team member. Make an agenda jointly so both parties are sure they are heard and there are no surprises.

Incorporate the human side of things too by doing the following:

At the beginning of meetings, ask everyone to rate their current wellbeing and let each member decide whether they want to talk about it.

For example: 'Today is not my best day, I feel like a two out of five, and I don't really want to talk about it.' This allows team members who are very private to feel understood. In such a situation, the others usually instinctively look out for that person, which means a lot to them. This is emotional safety without having to force your team members into unnecessary or vulnerable conversations.

Team building

Team building is an integral part of connection. Though the terminology sounds a bit outdated, with the changes in the post-pandemic work world, it becomes again an important task for mid-level managers. With so many people working in hybrid and remote scenarios, it is a challenge to 'build' a team and create that all-important feeling of belonging, trust and connection.

Here's a terrific example that none of your team members will even realise is an exercise in team building.

RECITATIVE: HILLY

Hilly, a very engaged organisational capability manager in the mining industry, had a team of around forty people. Most of them were enthusiastic and hardworking young people. She realised that there was a challenge for her as their leader. Individually, everyone on the team was excelling. But they could have worked better as a team and seemed very competitive, vying for their boss's attention and praise. The hybrid work arrangements that were in place did not help the current team situation either.

Hilly decided to address this issue by planning a team outing, but stayed away from team-building exercises that were competitive in nature. Instead, she chose an activity that highlighted the importance of a team in harmony.

Hilly asked her team members to come into a big room, where she invited them to play a three-round game.

For the *first round*, she asked everyone to pick up a balloon from a table, blow it up and write their name on it with the provided felt pens without bursting it. After the team members had done so, with lots of laughter and a few balloons exploding, everyone had to leave the room and wait outside for the next round.

After some time, she called them back to the room for the *second round*. Now balloons without names were scattered around, along with those with names on them. Hilly told her team members they had five minutes to find the balloon with their name written on it. The first three people to find their balloons would be declared winners. If someone busted a balloon, they would be disqualified.

Chaos immediately ensued as team members charged around the room, eagerly searching for 'their' balloon. Balloons flew everywhere and quite a few burst at the hands of desperate team members. After five minutes, Hilly stopped the round, and everyone had to leave the room again. By then, a few team members had been disqualified, but no one found the balloon with their name on it.

For the *third round*, Hilly changed the rules. She told them that if any team member found a balloon with any name, they had to give it to the person whose name was on it. Hilly gave them the same amount of time as before - five minutes.

The group was let into the room again, and everyone started searching. Within four minutes, everyone had found the balloon with their name on it.

Hilly said, *'No one could find their balloons as we worked on individual targets. But in the final round, within a few minutes, everyone had their balloon. That's the power of teamwork and collaborating.'* This was a landmark experience for the team, and from then on they worked well together, always supporting and encouraging each other. They all knew what was important to their boss, Hilly: a harmonious, collaborative team.

Mistakes

Resonance is not necessarily a pleasant sound. That comes later when a team moves into Consonance. So, when a team is in Resonance, guess what happens? Mistakes!

At this point, if you've followed my outlined steps, your team has established how they connect, work together and communicate. This is a bit like when a couple gets to know each other. They are loved up. 'Everything's so great!' Then they get to know each other better, on a deeper level, and suddenly, they are hit by reality. The honeymoon phase is over, and it's not all so great all the time.

It's the same with a team.

We start a job, and all is good. Everyone is so nice and supportive, the work is fantastic, and we learn so many new things. Then, after some time, we discover flaws and weaknesses in other team members, perhaps even within ourselves. We discover that mistakes are made, and we start feeling uncomfortable about losing the perfect picture.

I have put mistakes in our model at the intersection of Resonance and Dissonance. They are the reason why teams in Resonance can move into the vibration of Dissonance. Mistakes can become a stumbling block for you as a people-leader and your teams, and can get you stuck into never-ending Dissonance.

So, how do we address mistakes? Do we overlook the smaller ones? Do we address them the second they happen? Do we go for an 'objective' approach? Is it better to address them together as a group or only with the person who made a mistake?

Many leaders think that they have to be 'the perfect communicator': always knowing exactly what to say in any situation and to any person, and always having the most exciting stories to tell. We wish! The fact is that communication is a fluid process. And we don't always get it right. With my clients, I like to work with a concept I have developed to be more realistic about this.

I call it the Slip, Flip, Grip concept.

ARIA: SLIP, FLIP, GRIP

It's natural for a **Slip** to occur in our communication. After all, we are human!

It means that what we say sometimes does not land at the other end. As communication is a two-way street, we sometimes drive past each other or crash. The important thing is to realise when this Slip is occurring.

We understand that we can 'crash or drive past' for various reasons. Slips can be caused by:

- Another person's stress behaviour.
- A mismatch of communication channels.
- A lack of the energy required to keep communication flexible.

- A miscommunication on what was said instead of how it was said.

At this stage, it's important to have the *awareness* that our communication did not work out.

The next step is to **Flip**. We do something about the Slip. We don't just let it happen without setting an action for change. The Flip step gives us a chance to try out a different communication style and a different angle. We might change our words, tones, gestures and facial expressions to see if that works better and if our message now lands better with the other party.

Unfortunately, I often see people repeat themselves and continue communicating in the same, ineffective way. Or worse, they hammer down their message. Clients have said to me, 'I was clear and precise, I've explained it all in detail, and they still didn't get it!' In such a case, no Flip is happening. People assume that their communication preference is the same as others', and they have no awareness or knowledge of how to deliver messages in different ways.

When we Flip, our intention should be to reconnect with the other person. We might word things differently when we repeat our message. We can give a different energy to what we say. We can use different words, gestures and facial expressions. This gives us another chance to improve the conversation and be more successful.

When we Flip and still feel that the communication is not improving, we have to continue to Flip until we get a result. Once we have done the Flip and see that we connect better, we can **Grip** it by continuing to use that unique communication style with that person in the future. Then, communication will flow again.

So, when we switch from Flip to Grip, we make the necessary *adjustments*.

While working in the Area Management of Western Europe for a particular company, I had a particular challenge with one of the Country Managers. At that time, I wished I had known the different communication styles, and I wished I had developed the Slip, Flip, Grip concept. Our communication did run into cul-de-sacs! Neither of us saw each other's communication style in meetings as best practice.

We were often engaged in staff meetings, and the way we thought of how to run these meetings was very different. While I was very structured and factual, the Country Manager was more about having fun and finding creative solutions that involved what I felt was silly banter. The more I tried to bring the meeting back to the agenda, the more the Country Manager deviated to what I felt were disruptions.

Today, I understand that her communication preference involved more fun, more colourful language and more breaks for creative solution finding. And I would adjust my words, tones and gestures and allow flexibility in the meeting agenda.

With the SLIP FLIP GRIP concept, your communication will allow you to become more flexible, open-minded and correct. You will connect with team members, superiors and stakeholders with different personalities meaningfully and productively. It will also help foster a safe, compassionate and inclusive work environment.

SLIP, FLIP, GRIP

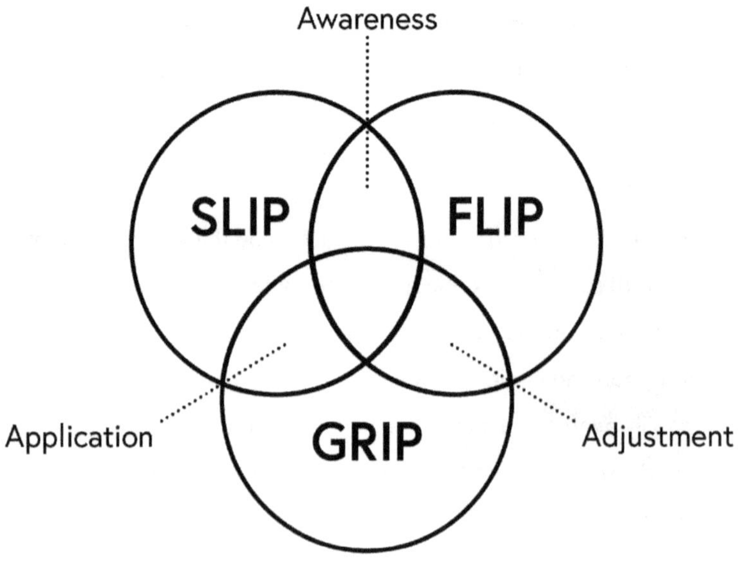

Mistakes happen in teams. I'd say they happen pretty regularly, in fact.

Many people-leaders take a positive approach and come from the thinking that we learn from mistakes. Despite this valuable mindset, mistakes often present grounds for disruption, disarray and disconnection. Emotions can run high, stress behaviour kicks in, and the team can drift into a hazardous form of drama and toxicity, which is much harder to come out from.

When and how errors are addressed is essential; if this is not done properly, it can sabotage the best intentions. People-leaders who see mistakes as a chance to enhance team communication and build stronger connections have the upper hand.

Mistakes encourage us to talk in greater depth about things and about what creates stress, and they highlight areas of focus. When this focus is held in a positive space, leaders can help their staff have better conversations. Leaders who can provide an agreed framework on how to speak about mistakes and how to correct them show a critical 'tuning tool' for team harmony.

So, you've used your tools for communicating and connecting to bring your team into a state of Resonance. But how do you know that it's working? Here are some signs that you are on the right track:

- You have lots of conversations to clarify things, set parameters and put structures around how your team works together.
- You laugh together, and your team forms good connections.
- New people are shown the ropes with extra attention, and they are integrated with compassion and care.
- You have a positive vibe and enjoy working together.
- You conduct team-building exercises.
- You practise communicating effectively in different 'languages' with your team members.

When you and your team have established a clear guideline for how you deal with mistakes, the Dissonance will be shorter. Everyone knows how to go about it. Yes, we know how to have those conversations that might be uncomfortable, but we move forward, not backwards.

When there is prolonged Dissonance within the team, it can wreak havoc. Let's talk about this in our next chapter.

ENCORE

- *Resonance* is how we come together as a team, whether hybrid, remote or in person. It is about establishing 'How do we go about this together, and make it work for all of us?'
- The main ingredients to achieve Resonance are strong communication and a connected culture.
- MMs who spend time on having their team in *Resonance* will be successful.
- Mistakes are unavoidable and can be difficult to manage. Still, they're also a sign of progress and an opportunity for growth.

ACT II

DISSONANCE

‘Compassion is the practice of demonstrating that people are valuable, capable, and responsible in every interaction.’

DR NATE REGIER

CONTRARY TO THE general belief that harmony only exists when things are peaceful, *Dissonance* is essential to team harmony.

How many teams have you seen without disagreements, different opinions or confrontations? The most likely answer is: none!

Four. According to 'Conflict at work', a new research report by The Myers-Briggs Company, that's the average number of hours per week managers spend dealing with conflict. The report shows that the number of people experiencing conflict at work often or all the time has increased by seven per cent since the same study was conducted in 2008. Yet, twenty-five per cent of people believe that their managers don't handle conflict well, allowing the friction felt in the workplace to snowball.

As discussed earlier, harmony in music is also composed of Dissonance, which plays a vital part in the overall perception of a harmonic tune. Without Dissonance, there is no resolution into harmony. In the case of a team, you may say there is no shift into a flow state or, as I call it, Consonance.

In this Act, we will explore what Dissonance is all about and why it is an integral part of team harmony. As the leader, you will have to deal with Dissonance quite often, especially in the beginning and middle phases of establishing team harmony. It is vital to look at techniques, tools and methods to give you the confidence to handle these more challenging aspects of leadership.

I will explain how you can shift your mindset around conflict and the importance of compassion. We will also examine how you and your team can combine showing compassion for each other with a strong sense of accountability. In my work with clients, initially, many leaders see those two attributes as opposites.

In the last part of this Act, we will look at the intersection of Dissonance and Consonance, which is where we find room for Experiments. It takes courage to experiment. In our work world, unless you work in research, we want guarantees that new strategies WILL work.

As you might imagine, Dissonance often occurs in teams

with flexible or hybrid work arrangements. Take my client Trent as an example...

RECITATIVE: TRENT

Trent is a B-level department head in a government body. Since the end of the final pandemic lockdown, his department has switched to a hybrid form of work, with parts of the team in the office three days per week, which they can choose. The rest of the team is completely remote, mostly due to their location, and they do not come to the physical office.

Trent is feeling exhausted after the past three years. He wants to work with his teams in harmony, as much for his own sake as theirs.

Burt and Sue are two of Trent's team members, with Burt being in the hybrid team and Sue in the remote unit. Trent sees Burt usually one day per week in the office, as their choice of weekdays doesn't overlap often. Trent had never met Sue before she joined the team, as she was hired during a COVID-19 lockdown, and he has had no time yet to visit her or other parts of the remote team in their respective locations.

Both Burt and Sue started to become difficult team members a few months ago and showed clear signs of stress and insubordinate behaviour, creating tension among their peers. Burt's constant questions in the meetings became more and more complicated over time, often not leaving any room for others to share their inputs. And Sue kept highlighting in Zoom meetings what everyone else should be doing and complained about the need for more professionalism and commitment.

Trent's attempts to intervene calmly and logically without addressing the behaviour did not have any effect. In what he thought were constructive one-on-one conversations, no solutions were found.

He knows that other team members were also affected, and he is afraid that they think he is not a capable boss.

The situation makes Trent frustrated. Deep down, he's thinking that Burt and Sue are constantly adding to his stress and workload with no end in sight. Although he likes his job and the responsibility that comes with his department, Trent finds himself contemplating quitting. His boss is understanding and supportive, but does not really do anything to help Trent. He feels left alone and stuck on a treadmill.

'Is this all there is to my job? Babysitting difficult people, with no resources to implement necessary changes to my teams, and constant drama? I am not a psychologist,' he keeps saying to his friends. But he stays quiet at work and does not discuss this openly with anyone.

How many of you are feeling like Trent? How real is this feeling of burnout, exhaustion and despair? I know that Trent is not alone. And I know that Trent needs help to get his team out of Dissonance and into Consonance.

In my work, we often deal with situations like Trent's, especially when new work arrangements have been put in place. For example, hybrid work is a flexible work model that supports a blend of in-office, remote and on-the-go workers. It offers employees the autonomy to choose to work wherever and however they are most productive, but it can also produce major hiccups in teams.

Identifying Dissonance

Many people-leaders and their teams go to great lengths to avoid conflict at work.

They have never learned how to deal with conflict in teams and do not know and understand that Dissonance is a normal part of teams and can be leveraged for good.

False harmony, or what many think to be harmony, tries to cover up existing energetic shifts. Doing something for 'harmony's sake' will encourage people to play only one tune to avoid Dissonance. That can become detrimental in workplaces and, counterintuitively, torpedoes authentic team harmony. After all, as much as you may try to avoid conflict, it is inevitable when you work in a team environment. Rather than preventing conflict or Dissonance, you must learn how to manage it and use it as a tool to bring greater harmony to your team.

Teams can display quiet but corrosive behaviour that can make the ship sink. In some company cultures, Dissonance is not welcome. I have heard executive leaders say, 'We don't do conflict here', while other companies discourage critical or inquisitive approaches as they do not want to foster disagreements.

Why is that?

People avoid Dissonance or deal with it inadequately because they do not know how to do this elegantly, damage-free and with a positive outcome. Rather than avoiding Dissonance, it's *crucial* to understand how to identify when it is happening.

I was sitting on a ferry once, travelling from home to the city early on a Sunday morning. Suddenly, I spotted on the grey horizon the silhouette of a submarine! In Sydney Harbour! I took a photo and started to think about how the main body of this submarine was under the surface, skimming through the water. And what I saw was only the fin and the periscope.

This reminded me of hybrid work and the dangers that loom under the surface for teams. The visible part of a team seems to cruise quietly through the water, but underneath, it can build a lot of undercurrents that can create Dissonance within the team.

ARIA: THE FIVE WARNING SIGNS

Here are five warning signs that may be present when your team is in Dissonance, along with the negative beliefs - which I like to call undercurrents - that team members might be privately harbouring when team harmony is in jeopardy:

1. Reluctance to speak out

People hold back. Inputs, critical views and challenges are not shared and discussed but swept under the carpet and dealt with silently. On the surface, it appears to be peaceful, but accountability is low.

Undercurrents

- Don't make any waves. Otherwise, the boat may capsize, or we may go overboard.

- I don't like arguments and avoid pointing out mistakes that impact work to avoid exposing anyone.

Counteractions

- Encourage open conversations in meetings.
- As a leader, share how you respond to a different opinion, so no one feels attacked or exposed.

2. Communication imbalance

The same individuals do all the talking, and the rest of the team is silent. Team dynamics seem to have led to an acceptance that some lead and others agree and follow. On the surface, it appears to be harmonious, but hidden emotions are smouldering.

Undercurrents

- If I don't talk, nothing moves forward.
- I must show my dedication to my job by leading conversations to progress in my career. Then, I can do my work in peace and remain undisturbed.
- I can avoid exposing myself by keeping quiet.
- I am not as bright as those who speak, and my contribution is not essential as we do just fine.

Counteractions

- Give shy and quiet team members the heads-up that you want their input on a topic in the upcoming meeting. Avoid generalising statements like 'I want you to participate more.'
- Gently influence the speaking time of each team member. Learn how to respectfully interrupt those who talk non-stop.
- Praise and acknowledge even the not-so-bright inputs. As a leader, you can ask good questions so the information becomes valuable. I love the motto 'Hold them high'.

3. Pseudo onboarding

No time is spent integrating the 'newbies' except friendly hellos. Everyone is nice on the surface. However, in reality the new members are seen as nuisances and time wasters, and the longer-standing team members don't want to invest any time and energy into helping them as there is so much work to do. The new people are expected to fit in as fast as possible. On the surface, everyone seems to be friendly with each other, but there is no team spirit.

Undercurrents

- It's too hard to explain things repeatedly to constantly changing newcomers. Why bother?

- If I do the work myself, I will be faster and more efficient and can cement my position.
- If I invest time in the new person, they might overtake me at some point, leaving me behind.

Counteractions

- Implement a buddy system.
- Give the buddy relief from some of their work so they see this task not as an additional workload but as a desirable and important role.
- Highlight the importance of being a teacher, and praise and reward the successful integration of the new colleague.

4. Chaos

There is little to no coordination of timelines, workloads and meetings; work seems to be ad hoc and built on individual initiatives. On the surface, it seems to be a good team flow, but there needs to be more clarity on working as a team.

Undercurrents

- I am so frustrated because I never know what's happening and who is doing what, but I can't share that with the others.
- I feel like I have to do all the work, and not everyone does their fair share.

- I do it my way. If you can't keep up, don't complain.

Counteractions

- Work with a team whiteboard (physical or digital) called 'working on the same page' or any name you want to give it that fosters teamwork.
- Write all the team members' names on the whiteboard.
- Every morning, or evening, ask team members to draw lines linking them to the people they have a current working connection with on the day. For example, 'I need your report by lunchtime to submit my final paper to the CEO.'
- When not met, connections might be highlighted in red the next day.
- This will help create an overview of what everyone is doing, and encourages fairness and transparency. When a team member is overloaded, others can help or assign work to other team members.

5. Cold atmosphere

No one speaks about life outside the work environment. It is unprofessional to spend time on small talk while at work. To be efficient, the focus has to be on the job, as there is so much to do and so little time. On the surface, it seems like a super-efficient team with a great work ethic, but there is no compassion and trust, and no space for being emotionally available.

Undercurrents

- I suffer in this cold environment, but I don't want to bother others with my feelings and emotions.
- I am happy that no one probes me about how I am feeling. I have no time for this touchy-feely stuff.

Counteractions

- Organise some (compulsory) social events with your personable presence as a leader. You might bring your family or partner to show a more private side. Please don't make it a drinking fest but engage in entertaining exercises.
- Run a 'what you might not know about me' round at the event.
- At work, share your feelings about work. The good, the bad, the ugly. Once people see that you, as their leader, are professional AND have a human side, they will love it and follow suit.
- It does not mean you have to bare yourself, but show your team that there is time at work for being human and getting to know each other.
- At the beginning of a meeting, let everyone give themselves a number (from one to ten) indicating how they feel that day:

only a number, no explanation needed. Team members can act on that number without knowing why. This especially helps people who do not want to talk about it to be emotionally present for others.

Many teams operate in the ways just mentioned and create toxic environments that appear free of surface friction. Especially in the new hybrid work environment, many undercurrents go unnoticed. For you as a people-leader, it is a good idea to pay extra attention to the signs.

Unfortunately, this is difficult to detect and can have the effect that teams are unproductive, not agile or badly equipped for the rapid changes at work.

So, how do you deal with those team dynamics, and how would you go about necessary changes? It is incredibly liberating when we know how to deal with Dissonance in the workplace. To do so, we have to lean into conflict and compassion.

In the rest of this chapter, we'll look at conflict and compassion, the twin pillars that are vital to dealing with workplace Dissonance.

Conflict

For you, as a people-leader, it is essential to know practical ways to deal with Dissonance, as it is inevitable in teams and your work environment. As I just mentioned, leaning into conflict is a key to dealing with workplace Dissonance. This may seem counterintuitive. Surely, it must be avoided so that we can maintain harmony. But as I hope you're beginning to understand, ostensible harmony can be an illusion that covers deeper problems. Conflict must be faced fully, and fearlessly, rather than sweeping it under the rug.

How do people react when conflict arises with the boss or within the team?

'When I'm forced into a difficult conversation I can't hide from, it consumes me and becomes very personal. It's really hard to shut out the bad feelings, and they take over so that I'll lose a whole day, fearing a difficult conversation. ... I fear conflict mostly because I fear shame. It never occurs to me that a conflict is about another person, us as a unit working together, or even based on a systemic issue.'

MORRA AARONS-MELE

Conflict in the workplace has a terrible reputation. But let's look closer at this. What is conflict?

What we associate with conflict are the disagreements ending in drama, the fights, the turf wars, the manipulation and the gaslighting. As leaders, we are often expected to handle conflicts within a team, which can drain us immensely. Think about it – conflict is quite a regular occurrence. Let's look at a work situation.

Peter is unhappy because his working arrangement has been shifted and he now has to come to the office four days per week instead of the previous three days. This messes up his and his wife's schedule of being able to pick up their kids from school. Peter has flagged this to his boss, and their conversation ended up being quite heated and left Peter feeling frustrated.

The situation is a typical example of a conflict, where the conflict per se can be seen as a gap. It is a gap between what Peter wants and what Peter gets. This gap creates tension, a feeling of friction, or you can say it's creating energy. So, Peter feels this energy, and his boss feels this energy. Now comes the crucial part: what do we do with this energy? And what are the results we get from handling this energy?

How we use this inevitable conflict energy determines whether we can make Dissonance work FOR team harmony or AGAINST it.

Most people do not like to feel this energy, and we often resort to unhelpful behaviour patterns to deal with conflict. What can you do as a people-leader to leverage the energy created by conflict in a good way that works for team harmony?

Let's look at a few scenarios that show how people deal with the energy the conflict gap creates. I invite you to think about what you currently do and what your team members do. Then consider how a mindset shift on conflict can help you deal with it positively.

1. Wasteful (avoiding the gap)

This is the scenario Morra Aarons-Mele explains in the aforementioned quote. Many of you have been in situations that caused rumination, sleepless nights, feelings of doubt, low self-worth and even physical symptoms of discomfort.

In this situation, you are trying to ignore or direct the energy against yourself inwardly, so you don't have to do anything out there in the world, like have a discussion or challenging conversation.

Mindset shift:

If this is you: It is worth addressing the conflict because I value myself. I am confident that a solution can be found. I will prepare well to address the gap and use the chance this conflict has created.

If you see this in others: Establish an atmosphere of safety and encourage an open dialogue. Indicate that you are here to hear them out and take their concern seriously.

2. Reckless (exploiting the gap)

In this situation, people misuse the energy for fear-mongering, aggressive or passive-aggressive manipulation, ghosting and gaslighting, often intending to gain a personal benefit. This behaviour contributes to and creates the often-mentioned 'toxic work environment' and leaves emotional scars. Words can hurt!

Mindset shift:

If this is you: It is worth revisiting my relationship with power and what is behind my behaviour. Is my gain really worth the damaged relationships? I can improve my emotional intelligence and understand how others perceive me. I will observe more.

If you see this in others: Set unambiguous behaviour guidelines. Don't sweep things under the carpet and let them go. Enquire what the motivation is behind the behaviour. Encourage coaching for this person.

3. Inefficient (closing the gap)

This can happen when people, companies and organisations want to 'go back to peace'. Mediation and conflict management are part of the culture. I remember when my boss in Beijing mediated a conversation between my colleague and me with little knowledge of how to do so. In the end, when the issue was dealt with merely on the surface, he made us shake hands and 'be friends again'. The conflict was nowhere near over, however, and the gap resurfaced immediately!

Mindset shift:

If this is you: I ask myself if I am clear on how to work things out. I will continue the conversation if I still need a clear plan with the other person. I will also ask for another check-in point so we know we are on track. Fix a date and time for this follow-up conversation now.

If you see this in others: Ask if everything has been addressed. Enquire about agreements and when the involved people will check in again to see if they are on the right track. Offer to attend this follow-up conversation.

4. Creative (leveraging the gap)

When dealing with conflict energy in productive ways, something new is created – such as a solution, an outcome or a step forward – and the dignity of all people involved is kept intact. The urge to drift into a drama, a justification loop or a defensive move is kept at bay.

Mindset shift:
If this is you: Congratulations!

If you see this in others: Congratulate them and observe if there is anything you can learn from them.

The ability to show empathy and be compassionate, and always have a positive outcome and a way forward in mind, will set you apart as a leader when dealing with conflict.

Steering those difficult conversations, and dealing with employee emotions, outbursts and withdrawals, can become easier with the right tools and practise. If you are a people-leader who takes on a role within a challenging work environment, you will have to deal with Dissonance a fair bit. Always know that you can do this!

This is the right time to learn good techniques to influence your surroundings positively. You can avoid taking things personally and keep up your energy. But it is not all on you alone. Educating your team members on those techniques is a great way to make them feel confident to deal with conflict well. This will have a profound influence on Team Harmony.

'The purpose of conflict is to create.'

MICHAEL MEADE

Compassion

An excellent way to deal with conflict is the Compassion Cycle©. Dr Nate Regier and his team at Next Element have explored, developed and tested this methodology, promoting what they call 'compassionate accountability'. The Compassion Cycle provides a safe way to communicate with openness, resourcefulness and persistence, and shows how you can lead with compassion and focus on accountability. It is my favourite tool to use with my clients to deal with stressful situations and difficult conversations. I am delighted to know Dr Regier personally, and I find his work invaluable in creating better workplaces.

Let me explain a bit more about what compassion is and why compassion, combined with a mindset of accountability, is a fabulous way of leveraging Dissonance in your team to create harmony.

The original meaning of compassion (Latin: compati) is 'to suffer with', indicating a willingness to lean into the suffering of someone else and the desire to find a way out of this suffering. So, if the suffering is a conflict, it is the willingness to lean into the conflict, use the energy positively and create a way out together.

In other words, we try to alleviate the suffering. Though we might not be clear about what happens after and how we are moving forward towards an outcome, accountability must come into play. If we combine the compassionate approach with a clear commitment from both sides on what to do next and follow that through, we have a winner!

So, the key to moving from Dissonance to harmony is a combination of compassion and accountability.

Are you all for compassion while neglecting accountability, or are you super accountable and neglecting compassion? If your leadership is focused on one of these areas, you might contribute to the Dissonance in your team, and everyone is left with a feeling that something is missing. Keeping a healthy balance is not always easy.

Let's look at the Dramaturgy Model, which I have created to help you move your team towards being compassionate and accountable. The model identifies four different leadership styles that indicate the levels of compassion and accountability displayed by the leader, who is ideally aiming to be the Developer. Following on from the model you will find descriptions that will help you identify which quadrant your leadership style falls into.

The Dramaturgy Model: Dictator, Drainer, Dramatist, Developer

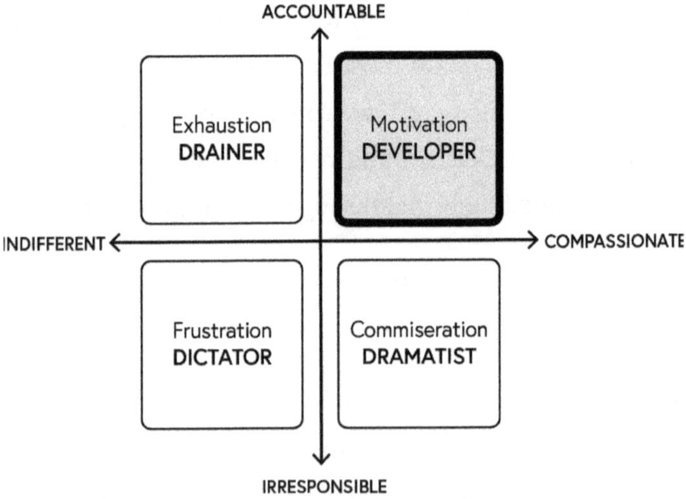

Dictator

Carina had been promoted to a team leader function during the pandemic. Deep down, she felt inadequately prepared for this jump but loved the pay cheque that came with it. She took on specific behaviour patterns she saw in previous bosses. She thinks that as a team leader, you must be tough and focus on others doing the work. She does not admit that she is worried and concerned that she will be 'found out'. That's why she covers this fear with an aloof attitude and does not give clear guidelines because she wants to avoid any conversations that might question work issues.

Things to observe:

- The leader is indifferent to the people in the team.
- The leader dictates what to do without following up.
- The people in the team don't collaborate.
- Team members work for their own advantage and try to survive.
- The environment is cold and chaotic.
- No one takes responsibility for the quality of their work.
- Everyone is frustrated.

Dramatist

When I was working with Richard, a very kind medical professional running his own practice with a team of sixteen doctors, nurses and admin staff, we established that he needed help with the many backlogs in the office.

Richard thought that listening and empathy were sufficient to motivate good behaviour. He avoided asking the individual team members directly to stick to deadlines and never discussed possible consequences when things were not done. He showed so much care and understanding for the consistent excuses, and there was always an atmosphere of 'it's all so hard to keep up' in practice.

While everyone said that Richard was 'such a lovely person', they did not respect him as a good leader.

Things to observe:

- The leader is warm and caring and understands life's hurdles.
- The leader sides with the team when things get tough.
- The people are compassionate and helpful.
- Team members are underperforming and limited in their productivity.

- The environment is kind and understanding.
- There is no sense of urgency; missed deadlines and targets are accepted as 'force majeure'.
- Everyone is stuck in a loop of commiseration.

Drainer

Peter ran a tight ship with his marketing team in an IT company. He was very proud of his functioning team, he made sure that everyone knew the compliance manual well, and he believed that rules were clear and consequences necessary to meet expectations. He made it clear that he did not want to hear excuses for why something went wrong or why a project deadline was not met. He simply refused to listen, especially if private matters were involved. From his point of view, they simply did not belong at work.

His staff had low morale, and they felt exhausted by constantly making sure that life did not get in the way of work, as well as the overregulated environment (death by compliance). No one dared to show weakness.

Things to observe:

- The leader is driving results and is married to work.
- The leader upholds deadlines and target performance as the holy grail.

- The people are high achievers and want to be perfect for the boss.
- Team members are reliable and tend to work overtime as the norm.
- The environment is cold and overly structured.
- There is no time for fun or human bonding. No one dares to admit to feelings that might show weakness.
- Everyone is exhausted.

Developer

When I was working with all three of these people-leaders, Carina, Richard and Peter, I asked them why things did not work for them. We looked at the concepts of compassion and accountability and the specific benefits that each leader would enjoy by combining them. We shaped a new communication strategy tailored to each client so that, step by step, they were able to implement a language that resonated much better with their team members.

All three of them showed great courage and the willingness to be open to trying out a new approach to tackle Dissonance. Today, Carina, Richard and Peter have their teams in harmony.

Things to strive for:

- The leader is goal oriented and gives all the necessary support to achieve the best outcomes.
- The leader is creating an emotionally safe and motivating workplace.
- The people are team players and support each other.
- Team members are successful and happy.
- The environment is one of learning and development.
- There is a sense of 'together we can do it', and no one is left behind.
- Everyone feels motivated and appreciated for who they are.

Far too many workplaces reflect a lack of compassion as well as accountability.

As a team manager, you know firsthand that it can become a vicious cycle when teams get stuck in Dissonance, when compassion is absent, and when no one takes accountability for their behaviour and actions.

So, how can you bring a team from Dissonance to harmony and Consonance?

If we look back at my core model, I have put *experiments* at the intersection of Dissonance and Consonance. To be a leader who is a Developer and knows how to motivate the team continuously, where all parties show compassion and accountability, it often takes some experimenting with different strategies.

As the examples of my three clients show, they were open to trying experiments. Working with a coach can help to strengthen the capabilities and get the necessary positive feedback to stay on track. A coach permits you to experiment! Parallel to this, involving the team to address new ways of communication when Dissonance occurs can be very helpful too. My compassion in conflict workshops help teams learn 'to dare to speak up' and 'how to tone it down' with a focus on positive outcomes.

I am incredibly grateful to all my clients, who often share very personal struggles with Dissonance in their teams. Doing so inspires people to be open, vulnerable and resourceful, and follow through on commitments. I have seen complete turnarounds, from chaos to cohesion, fostering my belief that team harmony is worth striving for.

Experiments

Have you ever felt that an experiment gives you a better feeling than a work project? There is something absolute with projects. They must work out. They have a fixed timeline. They often suck. With experiments, you get more of the feeling that you are allowed to fail despite all your efforts; there is a lighter connotation around an experiment.

If you can relate to this, you might want to try more experiments with your teams, and you might be very successful with them!

When it comes to addressing a conflict using an experiment, it's important to agree on steps forward and then try them out. If the experiment doesn't work, then you have to discuss it and try another approach. Eventually, through trial and error, you will figure out what works best for your team.

As you try different experiments with your team or team members, you may experience some frustration. Just remember:

- See the conflict for what it is – energy you can use for growth.

- Use this energy creatively to launch another experiment that you and your team leverage.

- Be accountable for what you do, whether your experiment goes well or not.

When your team is in Dissonance, you have a choice: you can turn conflict into drama or use it to create positive results. To find out if you've been turning conflict into drama, take the following self-check. If you tick a lot of the boxes in the first section, you can use the second checklist to help you overcome these tendencies.

ARIA: SELF-CHECK – DRAMA VS POSITIVE CONFLICT

Our socialisation and our wiring of the human brain naturally want us to turn conflict energy into drama. Drama is caused by clashing behaviours and personalities. A team is always made up of different people with differing personalities, so as a leader you have the challenge of understanding that different reactions can cause drama.

Here is a list of various behaviours that can turn a conflict into drama. This checklist allows you to do a quick check in difficult situations. What do you observe? Tick all the boxes for things you think that you are doing, or that you see your team doing.

Here's what people do that can turn conflict into drama:

- ☐ Avoid difficult conversations,
- ☐ Give in when they are pressured,
- ☐ Shut down when they don't feel heard,
- ☐ Display passive-aggressive behaviour to get what they want,
- ☐ Blame others for how they feel,
- ☐ Manipulate situations and people based on their ulterior motives,
- ☐ Use 'management by fear' tactics,
- ☐ Stick stubbornly to failing strategies,
- ☐ Burst into tears,
- ☐ Justify their position, and

- ❑ Stick to 'neutral facts' as if they are not involved.

You've ticked some boxes? Or only one box? Now let's look at what you can do more to shift the energy of conflict into the compassion and accountability direction.

Are you already doing some of these? Fantastic - keep doing them and reflect on whether you want to add some of the other options.

Here's how you can turn conflict into positive results:

- ❑ Empathise to make an emotional connection,
- ❑ Validate feelings without condoning unacceptable behaviour,
- ❑ Share emotional experiences that relate to the given situation,
- ❑ Ask curious questions and show interest in other people's perspectives,
- ❑ Look for commonalities to build on,
- ❑ Spotlight strengths and how they can help with the situation,
- ❑ Show flexibility when new information comes to light,

- ❑ Admit and accept your own mistakes,
- ❑ Be explicit about boundaries without blame, attacks or threats,
- ❑ Ask for improved and positive behaviours, and
- ❑ Learn how to give a good apology.

Learning how to use Dissonance to your advantage to grow your team is an important step to becoming a team in harmony. Regardless of the conflict you might identify within your team, creating an environment of compassion and accountability is most important when it comes to solving problems and growing from challenges.

Sometimes, it takes some experimenting to find the solutions for difficult problems, especially conflicts between team members, but being open, compassionate and accountable will help you and your team overcome every difficulty with grace.

Do you remember Trent, the department head in a government body struggling with Burt and Sue?

Working with Trent, we first established a quick analysis of where the team was and where he, as their leader, was. His team was in Dissonance, with Sue needing to be adequately onboarded and Burt not feeling recognised for his contribution. Both situations were snowballing on the rest of the team. After looking closely at his leadership communication potential (report and debrief), we discovered a couple of blind spots. Trent learned that his conflict with Burt and Sue was linked to these blind spots. We worked on tweaking Trent's conversations so both felt heard and newly motivated.

Then we started to focus on conflict, compassion and accountability. The entire team was attending a workshop on how to have good conflict conversations without damaging relationships and with a focus on moving forward. It was great fun for all of them, and Sue and Burt found the training very insightful.

Trent could see that the way Sue shared her concerns changed for the better, and he became receptive to her points of view. At the same time, Burt seemed more relaxed and stopped oversharing and over-qualifying his meeting contributions. That was a relief for everyone!

Trent made an extra effort to show more compassion for all his team members, checking in with them regularly to see if they had all they needed to work towards becoming an A-team. He also ensured that they followed through on what they had agreed on. He dealt with bottlenecks immediately and became a fantastic Developer (see the Dramaturgy Model).

After working with Trent and his team for eight months, with a range of coaching, workshops, team coaching and impact sessions, both in person and virtually, Trent was delighted looking at his team of Champions. Any thoughts of resigning had vanished, and he felt that he and his team were in harmony.

ENCORE

- **Dissonance is a standard and essential part of team harmony.**
- **Dissonance requires intelligent and strategic thinking in dealing with conflict and showing compassion and accountability.**
- **Embracing Dissonance leads to positive outcomes. It becomes easier with practise.**

- For any mid-level manager, this confidence and agility to deal with Dissonance is integral to good leadership.

- It is paired with a mindset that everyone in the team is valuable, capable and responsible.

ACT III

CONSONANCE

'It's got NOTHING to do with power. See, this bothers me about the perceptions of my profession that it has to do with power. It has as much to do with power as a musician playing the piano has to do with power. The orchestra is my instrument. I'm the pianist. The orchestra is the piano.'

SIMONE YOUNG

Chief Conductor of the Sydney Symphony Orchestra

So, YOU HAVE put in much work to have a grounded and rounded team.

They are in Resonance with each other. They know how to communicate well with each other, taking individual preferences and conversation styles into consideration. This supports everyday communication, and work flows well. You and your team members have built cognitive and emotional connections and are there for each other in good and bad times. Their ability to openly discuss challenges and personal 'pet peeves' without fear of recrimination or alienation moves things forward with a win-win mindset.

Your team also has learned how to handle Dissonance well. You and your team show compassion for each other without losing sight of accountability, and you have ditched drama and gossip for open discussions and solutions to disagreements. There is always time for the human in everyone. Your leadership is respected because of this quality.

How do we keep this up? What must we do so that this dream team is here to stay and continues to perform at its best? How do we keep our team in *Consonance*? This is where your leadership will be the guiding light. This is where your uniqueness as a leader will shape the territory.

It is like the conductor guiding the different sections of the orchestra. Sometimes the violins need more attention and practice in a particular section of the music piece. For example, sometimes the 'hand-over' of the main tune from the cellos to the flutes is clunky and needs focus. I am sure you have seen the conductor waving his baton, bending slightly forward and looking at the cellos, then directing the baton and his glance to the flutes. They ensure the musicians are cared for and no one drops out or is left behind.

The conductor knows when to take the lead, let go, and trust the musicians to understand how to play their parts well. They make sure the music keeps flowing and all instruments are in harmony.

In this chapter, I will look at two essential aspects of *Consonance*.

The first aspect is WHY it is important and beneficial. When a team is in Consonance, you also gain some excellent by-products or benefits. Firstly, you have a desirable work culture within your team. In addition, you and your team contribute positively to the overall company culture. Secondly, a team in Consonance is the perfect breeding ground for creativity and innovation.

With your leadership and the ability to fine-tune the *Consonance* of your team, you will be an essential contributor to a good work culture and a provider of an environment where creativity can blossom. Both are highly sought-after attributes in our modern business world, and companies with these attributes will find themselves on the awards list for 'Best places to work'.

The second aspect I will look at in this chapter is HOW to maintain it. What can you do as a people-leader to keep the team in Consonance and harmony? I will share with you some ideas on how you can do that. We will also look at soundchecks that help with that in the last part of this Act.

It is tempting to do less and less conducting when your team works like a perfectly functioning orchestra or runs like a perfectly oiled machine. Leaders who rest on their laurels and become overly content with their achievements will quickly lose team harmony and momentum.

So, it is vital for you as a leader to calibrate. In the modern workplace, we deal with change after change after change.

It is easy to get caught up in the everyday work that leaders forget to set time aside for maintenance, but it is essential to keeping your team in harmony and producing a positive company or business culture of creativity and innovation.

Team harmony is a prerequisite for innovation and creativity. Even if you and your team don't have an innovative task per se in your organisation, you will find that creativity is a nice by-product when your team is in Consonance. Your team will feel inspired to contribute to an easier work flow, implement new ways to collaborate with other departments and clients, and handle any changes much better.

Creativity and Cadenza[7]

Hardly any company or industry isn't keen on innovation and creativity. There are high expectations on you as the leader to manage teams in ways that help them come up with new ideas, solve problems and continuously improve their clout. In a nutshell, your teams contribute to the overall competitive advantage of their company.

Research shows that merely nominating people as a team (in this case, a creative team) will more often NOT give you the results you are after. In a study by McKinsey, it was found that eighty-four per cent of CEOs see innovation as critical to business growth, but only six per cent are satisfied with their innovation performance.

I would argue that there is no better way for you to foster creativity than by getting your team members into Resonance with each other, by knowing how to engage peers in open discussions, with the confidence of learning how to handle tricky and sticky arguments when the team is in Dissonance, and by observing how the juices will flow when the team is in Consonance.

It is hugely beneficial when your team is in Consonance and can achieve this. Some people believe that team competition brings about creativity. This is a short-sighted view because such an environment leads to chaos, burnout, and people leaving.

So, what can be done to get people working as a team together quickly? How can creative thinking emerge? How can the team leader foster such an environment?

This exercise encourages participants to think outside the box and come up with creative solutions by forcing them to combine seemingly unrelated ideas. It can be done quickly and easily in a team meeting or workshop and can be adapted for different group sizes and time constraints. And it will provoke much laughter!

ARIA: BRAINSTORMING MASHUP

1. Divide your team into groups of two to four people.

2. Ask each group to come up with a list of at least ten unrelated words or phrases (such as 'apple', 'moon', 'sunglasses', 'roller-coaster', etc.)

3. Once all groups have created their lists, ask them to share their lists with the other groups.

4. Now ask each group to randomly select one word or phrase from each of the other groups' lists (so each group should end up with two or three words or phrases that they didn't originally come up with).

5. Finally, give the groups ten to fifteen minutes to come up with a creative idea or solution that incorporates all of the words or phrases they were given.

For example, suppose one group was given the words 'apple', 'moon' and 'sunglasses'. In that case, they might come up with the idea of creating a new type of telescope that uses apples to magnify the Moon, with built-in sunglasses to protect the user's eyes.

Teams in Consonance will also do the Brainstorming Mashup exercise much better. They will feel free, safe and motivated to come up with the silliest suggestions and they will reach their goal faster.

So, your team is resonating. You are leveraging the creative and innovative effects of team harmony, but you can hear the drums of change and conflict in the distance. How do you protect all the work you and your musicians have done and keep them in *Consonance*?

This is when the importance of your team culture comes into play. In this next section, we'll explore ways to maintain a positive team culture that continuously fosters creativity and innovation, no matter what change or challenge comes your way.

Culture

A lot has been written about culture at work. As stated previously, a good work culture is the result of Consonance. But why is Consonance important? Well, conflicts and changes inevitably arise that can jeopardise team harmony. Having the right tools to address those changes and protect your team culture gracefully will ensure perfect Consonance (or the maintenance of team harmony). What can cause trouble and very quickly change an existing excellent team culture? New team players.

I have heard from people-leaders that they are often concerned when new staff join the team because they fear that an existing good culture and atmosphere gets disturbed. What they might have observed in the past is that with a new team member, things can change for the worse quickly.

When it comes to maintaining positive culture with the welcoming of new team members, onboarding is crucial, and many companies don't get that right. People-leaders are often not fully involved in that process and leave it to the HR or People and Culture department.

In many circumstances, onboarding involves handing out computers, passwords, and watching some training videos on the company values, the company history, and 'who is who' in the hierarchy. There will be a welcome within the team, and then ... nothing. One sits and waits to see how the new person fits in.

People-leaders keen to integrate new personalities into their existing great culture will have to actively get involved in the onboarding process.

An excellent way to do that is to address different communication styles. A culture is massively shaped by how we communicate with each other and how aware we are of different styles.

RECITATIVE: SVEN

Sven, a middle manager in a global bank, had a great team of thirty-three staff. They were very much in tune, collaborated well, and had a reputation as a successful team. Sven had worked hard to get the team where it was, and he was happy and grounded in his leadership.

Then along came Svenja, who had a big personality. She began to split the team immediately. Some found her entertaining and outspoken, and enjoyed the 'oomph' she brought to the shop. On the other hand, some found her terribly disruptive, loud and annoying. They felt the focus was no longer on achieving excellent team results, but on having fun and taking every opportunity to engage in group conversations.

Sven was not too happy about the choice of Svenja. He was outvoted by the interview panellists, who came from various departments. Though Sven had nothing against Svenja as a person, he could see that her personality would ruffle some feathers and could create friction.

Sven had put much effort into bringing his team to where they were: engaged, focused, happy and collaborative.

What he feared would happen did happen. He saw a rift emerging between his team members, and the Consonance was going down the drain. Though Svenja was good at her job, she disrupted a well-running workflow, and her sometimes chaotic, last-minute way of doing things was causing trouble.

'How can I regain harmony in my team and establish a healthy culture?' Sven asked.

When a new team member joins, it is important that the team has an opportunity to build Resonance with that new person so that integration under your leadership can happen smoothly. Using the tools from Act I, to establish good communication and connection between your existing team and the new person, will ensure harmony in no time.

When I worked with Sven and his team, we explored an understanding of new communication styles, including how different people react under stress and what the team members could do to motivate each other out of stress.

We looked into everyone's communication potential and where people had blind spots. Of course, the existing team members and Svenja had a few aha moments. However, the team fully embraced the new diversity. They learned how to speak about it when they felt interrupted in their work or misunderstood.

Sven was delighted. He had established harmony within his team again and enjoyed the fact that everyone, including Svenja, had built better relationships. Svenja's unconventional style was now seen as an asset rather than a threat.

I have written about communication in *Act I - Resonance* in detail. When new people join the team, and their way of conversing looks pretty different from others', it is a good idea to revisit what the team has agreed on in terms of how to communicate effectively.

As a leader, you will want to encourage an open conversation about team changes, how new communication styles have developed, and what new people can bring in to enrich future communication.

Dedicating some time to facilitate this discussion is a worthwhile undertaking. That can be in a meeting, a special team gathering, or a video call when you have a dispersed team. When you are optimistic about integrating new communication styles and encourage team agreements to adapt to new people rather than hoping they fit in, Consonance will be the result. These 'check-ins' are what I like to refer to as soundchecks – they are the HOW to achieve team Consonance.

Soundchecks

A soundcheck in the musical world involves all musicians to find out if everything is working and if their joint playing of the instruments has the desired sound effect. It is not a rehearsal but merely a check that all is well and that the musicians are prepared and ready for the performance.

A soundcheck is also good practice for a team. And not only when a new staff member comes on board but also as a general way of ensuring the team has what they need to work together productively and in emotional safety.

So, let's take a closer look at how you can maintain your team in Consonance amid changing working environments, priorities and team member dynamics.

Do you remember when you created the Team Charter in the Resonance phase? Here is the follow-up exercise I recommend regularly undergoing.

ARIA: CHARTER REVIEW (SEE ALSO ARIA: TEAM CHARTER)

In this exercise, you and your team assess whether the Team Charter is still effective or requires adjustments. This may be especially important with new team members or other changes to work arrangements. Follow these steps to complete a Charter Review:

1. Schedule a time for the team to come together to review the Team Charter, such as at the end of a project/experiment or on a quarterly basis.

2. Review the Team Charter together as a team and assess how well the team has been adhering to the Charter's agreements.

3. Discuss any challenges or issues that have arisen since the last Charter Review, and brainstorm ways to address them.

4. Update the Team Charter as needed, based on the team's discussion and feedback.

What else might you do to keep Consonance in your team?

Based on my experience in managing teams in my airline days, I believe in engaging team members in regular joint activities that foster relationship building and maintenance. This is especially important with hybrid work scenarios, where losing touch with each other is easier.

Here is a series of questions that can help you as a leader conduct regular soundchecks with your staff. Ask yourself:

- Is our infrastructure still supporting us? Do we have to make adaptations?
- Are we still in tune?
- Are we resonating?
- Where is Dissonance occurring, and who is involved?
- Do we need to practise a bit more where the hiccups are occurring?
- Do we need to provide some help or training regarding compassionate accountability?
- How can I engage the newcomer and my existing team on a deeper level so we put the whole team in Consonance again?

- Do we recalibrate our communication?
- Are we open to checking if our existing ways need a bit of fine-tuning?
- How do we involve the new team member so they don't feel they must 'fit in' but learn how to 'feel in' by being themselves?
- How can we get better at what we do together?

Soundchecks can be a fun thing. There is no pressure that immediate actions have to be taken, as there are no crises present. It is more a case of 'Hey, let's see if all is running smoothly, just to be on the safe side.'

Nonetheless, they are important and should be part of your work as a people-leader. Try incorporating soundchecks into your weekly team meetings to maintain consistency. Making Consonance fun will make it feel less taxing and more light-hearted.

Here is one of my favourite team spirit maintenance exercises, which can accommodate a hybrid model and include team members working remotely.

ARIA: SECRET PARTNER

This exercise helps foster and maintain a culture of mutual support and appreciation for each other. As a result, relationships are further strengthened, encouraging the entire team to collaborate continuously.

This is how you do it:

1. Give each team member a secret partner, and ensure that team members do not reveal who their assigned secret partner is.

2. Encourage acts of kindness. Throughout the day, each team member will leave notes of encouragement or small gifts, or perform acts of kindness, for their secret partner.

3. Ensure you find ways to support your secret partner without being detected. That might take some creativity, especially if your partner is working remotely.

4. At the end of the day, do a 'big reveal', in which each team member gets to know who their secret partner was and where everyone shares what touched them most. You will find a renewed strengthening of relationships, a deeper appreciation for each other and a boosted team spirit.

When teams are in Consonance, you will find that the culture improves and people are happy at work, less likely to leave the company and put in the extra effort when required.

Thinking back on my airline career, it felt good to lead teams that were in Consonance.

Each staff member was very clear about their role, cheered each other on, and we celebrated what we had defined as success. I facilitated regular get-togethers that allowed engaged discussions and meaningful connections. No topic was taboo, and we embraced our different views and work methods. We launched some exciting and creative engagements with our clients, and we had a trusting and beautiful way of dealing with human troubles that occurred from time to time.

Many years after I left Austrian Airlines, I met with some of my previous colleagues. In retrospect, I was deeply touched by their comments about my leadership. They said they always felt heard, their ideas and suggestions never got a no, and they felt safe and supported. They said the team was in harmony.

ARIA: CONSONANCE SELF-CHECK

How do I know when my team is in Consonance? Here are some signs that you and your team are achieving Consonance:

- You have a proven way of communicating with each other, and misunderstandings rarely occur.
- You enjoy being at work, in each other's company, and having a great time on Zoom calls.
- You address problems early and in a compassionate way. You find solutions and stick to them.
- Your team's success makes everyone feel deep satisfaction and gratitude.
- You cheer each other on and are generous with praise.
- You have lots of good ideas and inspire others with your creativity as a team.
- You do not rest on your laurels but keep moving and improving.

Consonance is worth the work, as it creates and supports what we see as good company culture and is an excellent base for creativity and innovation to grow from.

ENCORE

- When a team is in Consonance, creativity and innovation can be achieved.
- As their leader, Consonance is your reward for guiding teams through Resonance and Dissonance.
- Enjoy this vibration and stay attuned, ready to act when Consonance is disturbed.
- Set up a maintenance plan for yourself, so you don't become complacent.
- Do regular soundchecks.
- Observe how the work culture is enhanced and how it positively affects other departments, clients and stakeholders.
- Keep looking for new ideas, and better ways to do things, as you will find the creativity and innovation switch is turned on.

CURTAIN CALL

JOE, OUR MID-LEVEL manager we met in the Prelude, is a wonderful human being.

By nature, he is fully committed to doing a meaningful job. He wants to do good for his company and to lead people with dignity and the support they deserve.

And then comes the reality of our current, often hybrid, work environment.

Exhaustion after the pandemic, and too few people with too much work to do. Changes every day, cost cuttings, redundancies and hirings that disrupt the workflow. The list is long!

This can take a toll on the best intentions, and, without training, proper preparation and an intelligent toolkit, there won't be any relief in sight.

Are you like Joe? Do you have the same aspirations to lead a team in harmony?

But where to start?

The first thing Joe did was conduct a brief analysis of where he and his team were at and what part of the orchestra needed to be more responsive to his conducting.

Based on the three areas of *Resonance*, *Dissonance* and *Consonance*, he found that only part of his team was in *Resonance*, a majority was in *Dissonance*, and they were not experiencing any *Consonance*.

Joe looked at the most critical focus areas of *Resonance*: Communication and Connection. He decided first to find out about his communication potential concerning leadership. He discovered that many of his team members had a preferred way of conversation that he did not share. He also discovered that due to his stress levels, his leadership became too controlling, discouraging trust, and his striving for perfection contributed to his feelings of burnout.

Joe found these insights so helpful that he decided everyone on his team should better understand different communication preferences. He organised a workshop, which was great fun for everyone and enabled the team to find a new common language. That significantly impacted the meetings and helped build better connections between the team members. Every new team member was also given an assessment and debrief, which worked wonders for the onboarding process.

But Joe knew it was inevitable that there would be conflicts and disagreements on the horizon and that the rose-tinted glasses would not be on forever.

The next area Joe tackled was *Dissonance*. He and his team learned about the difference between drama and positive conflict. They shared their experience openly and why there were so many disagreements, instances of disobedient behaviour and gossip. This was a bit tough. Old wounds were opened, and the training seemed to disturb the newly gained team *Resonance*. Joe did not shy away from leaning into this process. He was open and vulnerable and gained tremendous respect from his team.

They worked through this phase over a few months by first learning how to have a difficult conversation with compassion and accountability and then practising the technique in a few shorter impact sessions. The team learned more and more about tolerance, willingness to hear people out, and finding strength not in pushing their opinion through, but in achieving a jointly agreed-on new goal.

Joe felt increasingly confident in addressing work problems without fearing objections or unpleasant reactions. And the individual team members learned how to get on with different personalities and accept other opinions without getting caught up in the drama. They also felt empowered to address issues without fear of being labelled as difficult.

Joe established regular check-in points with all of his staff to ensure that those outside the office or working remotely were fully connected, informed and visible. He promoted a mindset shift towards 'We love change because we can talk openly about all aspects of it.'

From then on, Joe felt he and his team went from strength to strength. His team always had unique solutions to challenges and was reliable in every work aspect, inside and outside the team. He became more relaxed, and there was no question with his superiors that Joe was doing a fantastic job contributing to the company culture.

Joe knew that this state of harmony still required regular maintenance, and he set up a plan for when to do what. He also knew that he had to look at *Resonance* and *Dissonance* when a new member came on board, or a significant change rippled through the organisation.

I hope that, like Joe, you will find a way through your difficulties by understanding the concepts set out in this book and employing the tools I have presented. Please share your successes, obstacles and team harmony with me!

I always love to hear from you.

ACKNOWLEDGEMENTS

I AM DEEPLY GRATEFUL to you, the reader, who took a chance on an unknown author and bought this title.

The idea for this book emerged through the long lockdown periods during the pandemic and the conversations I had with Matt, Richard and other mentors and students from the Thought Leaders community.

With the return to work, I started to see the many challenges leaders and mid-level managers face and how much the work world has changed, so I wrote a guidebook that helps them instantly with their ever-so-important roles.

I want to dedicate this book to my Mutti (mum), Hildrun, in Austria and my teenage son, Timmy, who lived with me during this process. He knows all about 'when mum has a fit about her book' and he listened!

My late father, Josef, would have been my biggest champion. I miss him every day.

My sister, Elisa, a decorated journalist, and her family were always here to help with inputs about the cover, title and problems people-leaders face in Austria. Thank you.

I could not have written this book without my book focus groups. A special thanks to Hannah and Daniela from my first group and Maria, Eleni and Faye from my second group. Your feedback was invaluable, and our time together will be with me forever.

I want to thank a few people, in no particular order, who always support me in whatever I do and never fail to inspire me. Thank you, Paul S, Moran, Andrea and Werner, Ken and Suryan from Work Club, Luzia and Reinhard, Barbara and Rashid, and Hannelore.

A wonderful house swap for ten days with my friend, Alanah, enabled a massive writing sprint, inspired by the beautiful tropical surroundings of Cairns, and the traction never left.

Kelly Irving and the Expert Author Community played a substantial part in my book journey, and Kelly's input boosted my confidence. She introduced me to the fabulous publishing team at Grammar Factory. A special thanks in particular to Scott, Olivia, Carolyn, Julia, Ania and Setareh.

Last but not least, I thank music and my upbringing in Austria for inspiring my concept and model for this book.

ABOUT THE AUTHOR

ILONA VASS IS an expert in leadership and team communication.

Ilona is inspired to improve how humans speak with each other and handle challenging conversations with ease and dignity. Her focus in training, coaching and facilitation is taking the pressure off communication for people-leaders, striving to build champion teams, and tackling challenges and changes with a positive outcome in mind.

She helps people-leaders discover and expand their full communication potential and teams to build an excellent everyday communication infrastructure, always keeping human originality in mind.

Ilona was born in Graz and grew up in Vienna, the music capital of Austria. Playing an instrument, regularly attending concerts, and attending 'die Tanzschule' (it was customary that all high school girls and boys attend a dance school to be instructed in ballroom and Latin American dances) was part of her upbringing.

Early in high school, she became curious about China's culture and language. She pursued her interest by studying a Master's degree in Sinology and Anthropology at Vienna University (founded in 1365).

After studying, working and living in China for many years, her interest in communication was stimulated as she experienced the many facets of intercultural communication in private and business settings.

In her first career at Austrian Airlines, Ilona held managerial positions, leading teams worldwide. She always pursued a collaborative and inclusive approach with teams and saw the benefits of working in harmony.

Her last posting with Austrian Airlines brought her to Australia, where she currently resides in Sydney with her son. Due to unforeseen personal reasons, Ilona had to switch careers and decided to use her experience and her interest in communication to undergo extensive professional development. She now runs her own practice, helping companies and individuals to better their communication.

She works with clients in Australia, Asia and Europe, offering a range of programs, workshops and retreats, including coaching, training, facilitation, mentoring and speaking at company events and conferences, both in person and virtually.

Ilona's work with clients strongly focuses on the new hybrid work forms' requirements and upcoming challenges with AI. She believes lifting communication capabilities and maintaining dignity in a team and multi-generational company environment is essential for success.

Ilona publishes regularly in online forums and magazines. She has co-authored the international bestseller *Elevate Your Life: The Most Inspiring Way to Take Your Life to the Next Level* (2016). Ilona is also a sought-after podcast guest and has occasionally appeared on SBS German Radio.

Connect with Me

Monthly newsletter

www.ilonavass.com/subscribe-newsletter

Website

www.ilonavass.com

LinkedIn

www.linkedin.com/in/ilonavass/

Conversation

www.bookme.name/ilonavass

Free resources

www.ilonavass.com/free-library

REFERENCES AND RESOURCES

5 challenges of hybrid work – and how to overcome them. Harvard Business Review. (2023, February 6). https://hbr.org/2022/02/5-challenges-of-hybrid-work-and-how-to-overcome-them

3 inspiring short stories about teamwork that you must share with your team. (2022, November 2). WinnersStory. https://winnersstory.com/short-stories-teamwork-1/

Breen, M. (2022, May 31). The new age of the middle manager. INTHEBLACK. https://intheblack.cpaaustralia.com.au/leadership/new-age-of-middle-manager

Christian, A. (2022, October 4). The non-linear workdays changing the shape of productivity. BBC Worklife. https://www.bbc.com/worklife/article/20220928-the-non-linear-workdays-changing-the-shape-of-productivity

Christian, A. (2022, November 28). How flexibility made managers miserable. BBC Worklife. https://www.bbc.com/worklife/article/20221123-how-flexibility-made-managers-miserable

Company, T. M.-B. (2022, October 18). New research: Time spent on workplace conflict has doubled since 2008. PR Newswire: press release distribution, targeting, monitoring and marketing. https://www.prnewswire.com/news-releases/new-research-time-spent-on-workplace-conflict-has-doubled-since-2008-301652771.html

Ddi. (n.d.). A race to retain high-potential talent – global leadership forecast 2023. DDI. https://www.ddiworld.com/global-leadership-forecast-2023/retaining-top-talent

Feuersenger, E., & Naef, A. (2011). If you want them to listen, talk their language: Communication, motivation and success in business and personal relationships using the process communication model. Kahler Communications Oceania.

Fostering team harmony. Human Kinetics. (n.d.). https://us.humankinetics.com/blogs/excerpt/

fostering-team-harmony

G., A. (2023, January 25). Parts of an opera: A quick beginner's guide. Musika Lessons Blog. https://www.musikalessons.com/blog/2016/11/parts-of-an-opera/

Great expectations: Making hybrid work work. Microsoft. (n.d.). https://www.microsoft.com/en-us/worklab/work-trend-index/great-expectations-making-hybrid-work-work

Growth & Innovation. McKinsey & Company. (n.d.). https://www.mckinsey.com/capabilities/strategy-and-corporate-finance/how-we-help-clients/growth-and-innovation

Guardian News and Media. (2021, February 4). Home workers putting in more hours since Covid, research shows. The Guardian. https://www.theguardian.com/business/2021/feb/04/home-workers-putting-in-more-hours-since-covid-research

How to kill a team's creativity. Harvard Business Review. (2014, August 1). https://hbr.org/2002/08/how-to-kill-a-teams-creativity

joshuacogar1. (2022, May 5). The importance of middle management in a remote workforce. Management Consulted. https://managementconsulted.com/middle-management/

Karseras, G. (2022). Build better teams: Creating winning teams in the digital age. FIU Business Press.

Katzenbach, J., & Smith, D. K. (2015). The wisdom of teams: Creating the high-performance organization. Harvard Business Review Press.

Lencioni, P. M. (2012). The advantage: Why organizational health trumps everything else in business. Jossey-Bass.

Lencioni, P. M. (2007). The five dysfunctions of a team: A leadership fable. John Wiley & Sons.

Matthew Turnbull, RCC. (2017, January 9). What is "team harmony?" LinkedIn. https://www.linkedin.com/pulse/what-team-harmony-matthew-turnbull-rcc-cima-cmfc/

Merriam-Webster. (n.d.). Resonance definition & meaning. Merriam-Webster. https://www.merriam-webster.com/dictionary/resonance

Orlick, T. (2016). In pursuit of excellence. Human Kinetics.

Regier, N. (2017). Conflict without casualties: A field guide for leading with compassionate accountability. Berrett-Koehler.

Regier, N. (2020). Seeing people through: Unleash your leadership potential with the Process Communication Model®. Berrett-Koehler.

Regier, N. (2023, July 12). What is compassionate accountability®?. Next Element. https://www.next-element.com/resources/blog/what-is-compassionate-accountability/

Resonance. Cambridge Dictionary. (n.d.-a). https://dictionary.cambridge.org/dictionary/english/resonance

Routh, Z. (2022, April 3). Zoë Routh Leadership Podcast: 256 A leadership code for building better teams from George Karseras. Apple Podcasts. https://podcasts.apple.com/au/podcast/256-a-leadership-code-for-building-better-teams/id1163003618?i=1000556250309

Lovric, D., & Chamorro-Premuzic, T. (2018, September 7). Too much team harmony can kill creativity. Harvard Business Review. https://hbr.org/2018/06/too-much-team-harmony-can-kill-creativity

Shambaugh, R. (2019, June 23). How to unlock your team's creativity. Harvard Business Review. https://hbr.org/2019/01/how-to-unlock-your-teams-creativity

(she/her), T. A. C. (2019, August 29). How to disrupt false team harmony. LinkedIn. https://www.linkedin.com/pulse/how-disrupt-false-team-harmony-tara-a-collison-ph-d-pcc/

Sound check. Cambridge Dictionary. (n.d.-b). https://dictionary.cambridge.org/dictionary/english/sound-check

Williams, Dr. M.E. (n.d.). Achieving harmony and increasing empathy. Psychology Today. https://www.psychologytoday.com/au/blog/the-art-and-science-aging-well/201612/achieving-harmony-and-increasing-empathy

Tanveer Naseer. (2020, January 6). 3 principles for creating team harmony in today's fast-paced workplaces. https://www.tanveernaseer.com/

how-to-maintain-team-harmony-in-face-of-changing-team-dynamics/

Why being a middle manager is so exhausting. Harvard Business Review. (2017a, March 22). https://hbr.org/2017/ 03/ why-being-a-middle-manager-is-so-exhausting

Why conflict is necessary and how to manage it (with Amy Gallo). Harvard Business Review. (2021, October 18). https://hbr.org/podcast/2021/10/why-conflict-is-necessary-and-how-to-manage-it-with-amy-gallo

Williams, P. (2020). Becoming antifragile: Learning to thrive through disruption, challenge and change. Hambone Publishing.

ENDNOTES

1 *Overture* comes from the Latin word 'apertura'. It is the instrumental opening of an opera.

2 Psychological safety: team members don't have to fear negative consequences when they ask questions, make mistakes, or express ideas and concerns.

3 The 'Human Equation' is the factor of human strength or weakness that needs to be considered in predicting the outcome of any social, political, economic or mechanical process operated by human agency. In other words, when promoted you have not been prepared for the 'human side of things', which influence you every day in your job. Before it was not your responsibility to manage this.

4 In opera, *libretto* refers to the text of the work being produced or another long vocal work. Libretto is a collection of texts sung to form an opera.

5 *Aria* is a solo melody performed with accompaniment during the body of the opera.

6 *Recitative* is a musical declamation sung in the rhythm of ordinary speech to propel the narrative or dialogue aspect of an opera.

7 A *cadenza* is a virtuoso solo passage inserted into a movement in a concerto or other musical work, typically near the end.